T0339725

Cambridge Elements ≡

Elements in Politics and Society in Latin America
edited by
Maria Victoria Murillo
Columbia University
Tulia G. Falleti
University of Pennsylvania
Juan Pablo Luna
The Pontifical Catholic University of Chile
Andrew Schrank
Brown University

THE POST-PARTISANS

Anti-Partisans, Anti-Establishment Identifiers, and Apartisans in Latin America

Carlos Meléndez
Universidad Diego Portales, Santiago, Chile

CAMBRIDGE
UNIVERSITY PRESS

Shaftesbury Road, Cambridge CB2 8EA, United Kingdom

One Liberty Plaza, 20th Floor, New York, NY 10006, USA

477 Williamstown Road, Port Melbourne, VIC 3207, Australia

314–321, 3rd Floor, Plot 3, Splendor Forum, Jasola District Centre, New Delhi – 110025, India

103 Penang Road, #05–06/07, Visioncrest Commercial, Singapore 238467

Cambridge University Press is part of Cambridge University Press & Assessment, a department of the University of Cambridge.

We share the University's mission to contribute to society through the pursuit of education, learning and research at the highest international levels of excellence.

www.cambridge.org
Information on this title: www.cambridge.org/9781108717366

DOI: 10.1017/9781108694308

© Carlos Meléndez 2022

This publication is in copyright. Subject to statutory exception and to the provisions of relevant collective licensing agreements, no reproduction of any part may take place without the written permission of Cambridge University Press & Assessment.

First published 2022

A catalogue record for this publication is available from the British Library.

ISBN 978-1-108-71736-6 Paperback
ISSN 2515-5253 (online)
ISSN 2515-5245 (print)

Cambridge University Press & Assessment has no responsibility for the persistence or accuracy of URLs for external or third-party internet websites referred to in this publication and does not guarantee that any content on such websites is, or will remain, accurate or appropriate.

The Post-Partisans

Anti-Partisans, Anti-Establishment Identifiers, and Apartisans in Latin America

Elements in Politics and Society in Latin America

DOI: 10.1017/9781108694308
First published online: August 2022

Carlos Meléndez
Universidad Diego Portales, Santiago, Chile
Author for correspondence: Carlos Meléndez, carlos.melendez@mail.udp.cl

Abstract: Where party identification is in decay or in flux, alternative political identifications have gained centrality. In this Element, the author develops a typology of post-partisan political identities: alternative ways in which rejection of or the absence of partisan politics is defining political identifiers or nonidentifiers. Based on the original evidence collected through opinion polls in different Latin American countries, as well as applying an innovative measurement, the author shows the respective magnitudes and ideological composition of anti-partisans (individuals who hold negative partisanships: strong identities based on predispositions against a specific political party or movement), anti-establishment identifiers (individuals who hold many negative partisanships simultaneously), and apartisans (individuals who lack any positive or negative partisanships). This Element demonstrates the usefulness of employing these categories in order to better understand different levels of party-system institutionalization, party-building, and partisan polarization in the region.

This Element also has a video abstract: www.cambridge.org//
PoliticsandSocietyinLatinAmerica_Meléndez_abstract

Keywords: partisanship, political identities, political parties, political disaffection, populism, party systems

© Carlos Meléndez 2022

ISBNs: 9781108717366 (PB), 9781108694308 (OC)
ISSNs: 2515-5253 (online), 2515-5245 (print)

Contents

Não estou vendendo a minha alma ao diabo

(I'm not selling my soul to the devil)

Former Brazilian President Fernando Henrique Cardoso denies automatic support for PT's presidential candidate Haddad, and confirms that he will not vote for Bolsonaro in the 2018 Brazilian ballotage

October 13, 2018. O Estado de S. Paulo

If you are confronted with two evils, thus the argument runs, it is your duty to opt for the lesser one . . . the weakness of the argument has always been that those who choose the lesser evil forget very quickly that they chose evil.

Hannah Arendt, Responsibility Under a Dictatorship

Introduction

In February 2018, Brazilians still did not know if Lula da Silva would be able to run for president again or would remain in prison with his political rights suspended due to judicial allegations of corruption. Eight months before the first round of the presidential elections, uncertainty reigned. Pollsters conducted surveys with two different scenarios: with and without Lula in the ballot box. In the first case, Lula obtained between 34 percent and 37 percent of the total votes, twice the support of his runner-up, Jair Bolsonaro, a federal deputy for Rio de Janeiro state. In the second case, blank and null votes rose from 8 percent to 32 percent, surpassing Bolsonaro's own support. An important share of the electorate did not know who to vote for, but most of them were completely sure about whom not to endorse. Considering the lesser-of-two-evils logic, Brazilians, like former President Fernando Henrique Cardoso, doubted until the very last moment.

During that month, Datafolha, a prestigious pollster, asked Brazilians whom they would never vote for. Every respondent had an answer. Lula had the most rejection among the presidential candidates, with 40 percent saying they would never vote for him, followed by Jair Bolsonaro with 29 percent. Then came Geraldo Alckmin (a former governor of São Paulo state and member of Partido da Social Democracia Brasileira [PSDB]) with 26 percent, Marina Silva (former presidential candidate and leader of Rede Sustentabilidade [REDE]) with 23 percent, and Ciro Gomes (a well-known politician from Ceará and leader of Partido Democrático Trabalhista [PDT]) with 21 percent. Journalists and pundits had by then talked about anti-petismo, defined as a solid animadversion against the Partido dos Trabalhadores (PT), a leftist party that had been in power between 2003 and 2016. The PT eventually became one of the parties most responsible for the Lava Jato corruption scandal, which revealed structural corruption in the political and economic system that had prevailed until then. But, as is evident, the rejection of PT only partially explains the strong disaffection toward the whole political elite. A significant proportion of Brazilians rejected not only PT's leaders, but also others belonging to established political parties like PSDB, Movimento Democrático Brasileiro (MDB), and PDT, and even relatively new political organizations like REDE. Therefore, there are reasons to think that the eventual rise of Jair Bolsonaro was a phenomenon not only explained by anti-petismo, but also more precisely by the hatred for the whole political establishment.

In the end, Lula da Silva was banned from running for the presidency, and PT replaced him as candidate with Fernando Haddad, who served as mayor of São Paulo between 2013 and 2017. Haddad went on to come in second with 29.3 percent of the valid votes in the first round. Despite the absence of its historic leader, PT maintained a solid following, enough to qualify to the ballotage. Haddad's electoral support can be explained by PT's partisanship, which survived the impact of corruption scandals. Identification with PT turned out to be resistant, solid, and vivid, as well as amendable to continuing to support candidates other than Lula. While in other Latin American countries partisanships have not been able to outlive corruption scandals – like aprismo in Peru – PT showed its strength as an identification that has conquered the hearts and minds of an important number of Brazilians.

However, (positive) partisanship by itself cannot explain the surprising rise of Jair Bolsonaro, an eighteen-year federal deputy who alternated between relatively small political parties and ended up nominated by Partido Social Liberal (PSL) as its presidential candidate. In previous elections for the Chamber of Deputies, PSL did not reach 1 percent of the valid vote, and its previous presidential candidate (Luciano Bolívar in 2006) got 0.06 percent of the vote. Noticeably, electoral support in favor of Jair Bolsonaro did not come from a positive partisanship but from anti-partisans, individuals who hold negative partisanships – against PT and against most other political parties that had forged the Brazilian partisan establishment (PSDB and MDB). In this Element, I will refer to those individuals who hold simultaneous and parallel negative partisanships related to the traditional party system as anti-establishment identifiers, as holders of a type of post-partisan identification that can help researchers to understand not only Brazilian politics, but also all other party systems where positive partisanships are in decay.

Partisan loyalties have eroded across a wide set of nations in recent decades. The specialized literature has detected significant partisanship decline in the United States and in many Western democracies. Researchers have categorized this phenomenon as partisan dealignment, a persistent pattern of ever-weaker political parties and a reduction in partisan identification (Dalton & Wattenberg 2002). The breadth of this phenomenon speaks to a general process that exceeds idiosyncratic explanations. In fact, factors weakening party identification in established democracies are also affecting emerging democracies (Dalton & Weldon 2007). Apparently, we are moving onto a scenario in which partisan fidelities are becoming less relevant for connecting citizens to public affairs, especially in the developed world.

In Latin America, the diagnosis of partisanship is mixed: While citizens' attachments to political parties have declined severely in some countries, in others they have increased (Lupu 2015a). Fragmented and fluid party systems have prevented the institution of a partisan establishment in many countries, which has reduced the likelihood of mass partisanship. However, evidence suggests that in some countries new political formations have successfully emerged, conquering the hearts and minds of the public (e.g. PT in Brazil), and in others, political parties have survived democratic interruptions while maintaining the loyalty of a share of the electorate (e.g. peronismo in Argentina). Nevertheless, lower levels of party-system institutionalization (PSI) have challenged the centrality of political parties in the public arena in this region (Mainwaring et al. 2018).

Partisan dealignment in many developed countries and partisan fluidity in developing nations oblige the academic community to try to explain how political identities work in post-partisan scenarios: those characterized by the loss of parties' capacity to connect individuals with their political agenda. The lack of awareness on this topic has made scholars describe this situation as "a void" (Mair 2013). But if partisanship is in decay in many countries, or at least has lost its centrality to explain political attachments, what has replaced conventional partisanship? What type of political identification has emerged in arenas where partisan loyalties are falling and/or having difficulties to deepen roots in society?

So far, we have two possible answers to these inquires. On the one hand, we should note the rise of negative partisans (or anti-partisans) to complement the picture of (positive) partisan decay. In Western democracies and in Latin America, an emerging literature has paid attention to a previously unattended side of partisanship. Negative identifiers – individuals who reject specific political parties – are as relevant as partisans in order to understand how politics works nowadays (e.g. Abramowitz & Webster 2018). On the other hand, evidence shows that former partisans in the United States have become "independents" (e.g. Klar & Krupnikov 2016). The decline of partisan identifiers in the United States has nurtured a group of educated and well-informed individuals unconnected with parties. In other countries, "independents" have a different profile: apathetic to political affairs and indifferent to political parties. These individuals, autonomous from parties, are labeled "apartisans" to emphasize their lack of positive partisan identities. A genuine nonpartisan, however, should also lack negative partisanship. In this Element, I use apartisans and nonpartisans interchangeably to represent those individuals who do not hold any positive or negative party ID.

In addition to "anti-partisans" and "apartisans," a third additional category should be included in the analysis of arenas in which traditional (positive) partisanships are in demise: anti-establishment political identity. In those scenarios where the political establishment is well defined and recognizable for most citizens, individuals might develop negative attitudes toward it, without endorsing any emerging political party. They might define themselves as "independents" (Klar & Krupnikov 2016), but they are not authentic apartisans because they do in fact hold multiple negative partisanships. Anti-establishment identifiers are those individuals who are characterized by their loathing of the main political parties of their party system.

I propose a typology that integrates these three nonpositive partisanships into a broader perspective. Based on previous empirical work, and expanding the breadth of analysis to several Latin American cases, I suggest that in order to understand individuals' hearts and minds, we should consider – besides positive partisanship – at least three more relevant political identities: negative partisanship (or anti-partisanship), anti-establishment identity, and apartisanship (or nonpartisanship). These three distinct categories are useful for understanding a variety of connections (and disconnections) between citizens and the public sphere, in contexts where positive partisanship is losing influence. While the literature normally has lumped together individuals who lack positive partisanship into a sole group (e.g. apartisans), I propose to separate different profiles among them. By understanding the nature of these post-partisan political identities, we can detect the type of political linkages based on their rejection of specific political parties (negative partisanship), their rejection of multiple political parties (anti-establishment identities), and the lack of any political linkage, which is the absence of positive and negative partisanships. What I mean by post-partisan political identities are the alternative ways in which rejection of or the absence of partisan politics are defining identifiers or non-identifiers, I exclude from the analysis societal identifications that might have been politicized (e.g. ethnicity) but which are not originally linked to political parties in their formations.

Latin America is an appropriate region to study these sets of political identities. From the standpoint of the public, partisanship is a measure of PSI (Dalton & Weldon 2007). And in this continent, we find a great variety of levels of PSI (Mainwaring et al. 2018) that I will address based on its schemes of (non)partisanships: institutionalized (but socially uprooted) party systems (e.g. Chile), very low levels of PSI (e.g. Peru), increased institutionalization (e.g. Brazil), and deinstitutionalization (with signs of recovery) (e.g. Argentina). I will demonstrate through original data gathered from surveys the diverse configurations of post-partisan political identifications according to different levels of PSI. By linking political identities with party-building, partisan polarization, and PSI, empirically and comparatively, I will contribute to the understanding of the fate of political parties in the region, and its consequences for democracy.

This Element is organized into five sections. In Section 1, I discuss the conceptualization of partisanship and present an alternative measurement that can allow us to tackle the different types of partisanships and what I refer to as post-partisan political identities (negative partisanship, anti-establishment identity, and apartisanship). The typology is exemplified empirically in the cases of Chile and Brazil. In Section 2, I develop in detail the conceptualization of negative partisanship and present the respective measurements of negative partisanships in seven Latin American countries. I focus on Peru as an example of a democracy with negative partisans. In Section 3, I approach the conceptualization and measurement of anti-establishment identification and apartisanship, clarifying common confusions between these two concepts. I tackle the cases of Chile, Brazil, Honduras, and Argentina to exemplify the main points. Moreover, I explain how anti-establishment identifications tune in with populist appeals. In Section 4, I address some implications of the perspective of post-partisan political identities to shed light on relevant topics of the study of political parties, such as party-building, partisan polarization, and PSI. Section 5 presents concluding remarks, pointing out possible paths to deepen a research agenda.

1 Conceptualization, Measurement, and Typology

Partisanship has been considered to be one of the most important variables to shape political attitudes, electoral preferences, and political behavior. When originally conceived, party identification was understood as an affective multi-dimensional orientation, that is, a positive and/or negative identification toward political parties, with some degree of intensity (Campbell et al. 1960). It has been comprehended as an enduring psychological affinity toward a partisan referenced group, similar to a religious identification (Green et al. 2006). Enduring partisan identifications are arranged considering the natural individuals' psychological reflexes to build boundaries, by perceiving themselves as members of an "in-group" and nonmembers as members of an "out-group" (Huddy 2001). As a result of this, socially rooted partisan identifications are based on shared characteristics among in-group members and in opposition to groups to which they do not belong (Bankert 2021). In addition to the social identity framework developed, a more pragmatic perspective understands partisanship as a "running tally" of retrospective evaluations of public administrations (Fiorina 1981). However, while the latter might be useful in explaining short-term endorsements of political parties, it is very limited to elucidate a more complex panorama of multiple and simultaneous types of (positive and negative) partisanships and their absence.

I build the proposed typology based on two original anticipated types of partisanship: positive and negative. Although seminal works have defined partisanship in these terms, the specialized literature has especially focused on the former. I consider that this is due to the fact that most previous research on partisanship has studied institutionalized party systems, settings in which positive and negative partisanships tend to overlap. In a hypothetical bipartisan background, most individuals who endorse party A simultaneously reject party B (and vice versa), and few individuals exist outside of those two groups (Figure 1). For this reason, focusing on the positive dimension of partisanship might have been sufficient for explaining political outputs.

However, this situation is no longer helpful when partisan politics is in decline (or in multiparty system settings). As important as understanding partisanship as the conquering of hearts and minds, is to understand political identities shaped by the visceral feelings triggered by parties (Medeiros & Noel 2013). Negative partisanship could be an autonomous construction (from its positive counterpart) since negative sentiments are not simply the polar opposites of positive ones (Medeiros & Noel 2013). Some people might develop only negative partisan attitudes, independently from positive attachments to parties

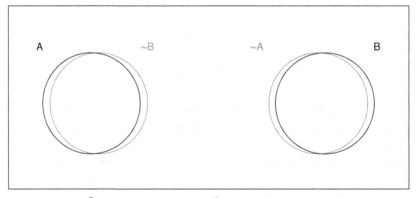

⃝ Positive Partisanship   ◯ Negative Partisanship

Figure 1 Institutionalized two-party system

(Haime, A. & Cantú, F. 2022; Samuels & Zucco 2018). That means strong out-group hostilities can develop without equally strong in-group leanings (Bankert 2021). Thus, negative and positive partisanships may have different origins, especially in low-institutionalized party systems, in which negative partisans exceed the decreasing scopes of positive partisans (Figure 2).

Moreover, it is possible that individuals could hold multiple negative partisanships (anti-E area in Figure 3). In the context of political disaffection, where individuals develop critical attitudes toward politics and representative institutions (Torcal & Montero 2006), they could reject simultaneously more than one political party, especially if these political parties belong to a discredited political establishment. This extreme situation – of strong criticism of the partisan establishment – has been very common in Latin America. An extreme case of feeble institutions and party-system collapse – the massive reduction of partisanship from all the established parties – has occurred in several Latin American countries (Morgan 2011; Seawright 2012) and in other regions of the world (e.g. Italy). Under this situation, individuals might have developed an anti-establishment political identity based on the simultaneous aversion to the then-mainstream political parties (Figure 3).

It is important to distinguish an anti-establishment political identity from a positive identification toward an anti-establishment party (Schedler 1996; Abedi 2004). While the former is an aversion toward the establishment that is not captured by any political party, the latter is the case of anti-systemic feelings channeled into a political project. I am interested in the nonorganized version of disaffection because it better expresses, in its natural version, the "anti-political" ideology (Schedler 1996). It is feasible to think that the development

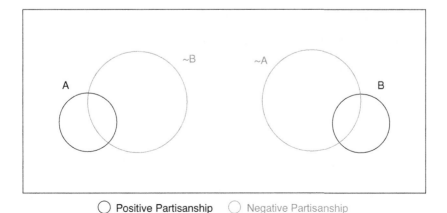

○ Positive Partisanship   ○ Negative Partisanship

Figure 2 Noninstitutionalized two-party system

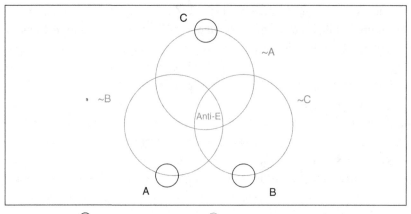

Positive Partisanship   Negative Partisanship

Figure 3 Party-system collapse

of an anti-establishment political identity might be a factor leading to the emergence of a populist leader (Meléndez & Rovira 2019) or for the occurrence of a party-system collapse. Based on this importance and the corresponding gap in the literature, I consider it relevant to include this profile among the post-partisan political identities.

Finally, apartisans compose a third profile of post-partisan identification. Individuals who lack any positive or negative partisanship belong to this group. This definition goes in line with that of Samuels and Zucco: individuals who lack a strong identification with in-group and lack a strong antipathy for out-group (Samuels & Zucco 2018). In this sense, this category is different from Dalton's definition that considers "apartisans" as all those independent from positive partisanships (Dalton 2013). I sustain that a rigorous definition of apartisanship should be separate from any type of identification with positive or negative partisanship.[1] Individuals who fall in this category are not attached in any way to politics, and express indifference toward the partisan offer. This is a separate group from those who reject a specific political party (anti-partisans or negative identifiers) and from those who refuse the established political parties (anti-establishment identifiers).

1.1 Measurement

The measurements of party identification have attempted to better capture partisan loyalty. In American politics, a conventional seven-point scale has

---

[1] I prefer the term "apartisan" instead of "non-partisan." The former better expresses the lack of any positive or negative partisanship; the latter normally involves the absence of positive partisanship.

been extensively used to grasp individuals' partisan alignments and the strength of their partisanship. The Standard American National Election Studies survey simply asks: *"Generally speaking, do you think of yourself as: a Republican, a Democrat, an Independent, or what?"* Then, the respondent is asked to call himself or herself a strong or not-very-strong Republican or Democrat. If he or she claims to be Independent, then he or she is asked if he or she thinks of himself or herself as closer to any of the two partisan options. After these questions, measures of party identification in the United States cover seven categories: Strong Democrat, Weak Democrat, Independent Leaning Democrat, Independent, Independent Leaning Republican, Weak Republican, and Strong Republican. Obviously, this measurement scale was created based on idiosyncratic considerations and has worked accurately for two-party systems.

Public opinion researchers have devised measurements of partisanship for Western democracies with pluri-party systems. For example, the European Social Survey (ESS) and the Comparative Study of Electoral Systems (CSES) have employed alternative wordings in this realm. They have focused on "closeness" to political parties in order to grasp individuals' leanings to political alternatives. The ESS's question asks: *"Is there a particular political party you feel closer to than all the other parties?"* The CSES asks in a similar way: *"Do you usually think of yourself as close to any particular political party? Which party is that? Do you feel very close to this party, somewhat close, or not very close?"* Both studies employ closeness to political parties as proxies for partisanship.

In Latin America, public opinion research has asked respondents directly about party identification or party sympathies. For example, the Americas Barometer's questionnaire includes the following question: *"Which political party do you identify with?"* This simple question has been employed to research mass partisanship in the region. Besides the relatively young age of democracies and, consequently, the high number of new political parties in these countries and the frequent party fragmentation, evidence shows that "some form of mass partisanship has emerged" (Lupu 2015a, p. 234).

The main disadvantage with these wordings is that they are "softer" measures of partisanships. First, one-dimensional partisanships do not capture the possible distinction between positive and negative party identifications, neither a combination of them (Weisberg 1980; Bankert 2021). Moreover, in some contexts, partisanship can be socially stigmatized, and direct questions on partisan affinities might suffer from social desirability biases. On the basis of these weaknesses, I have proposed a more rigorous and "thicker" measurement of partisanship, based on the original idea of partisanship as party loyalty, and considering the challenges of electoral volatility and party fragmentation that characterizes weakly institutionalized party systems. Thus, the proposed measure tackles a strong partisan loyalty expressed in the form of a committed and engaged voter who will vote for the same party regardless of the level involved. This proposed measurement is also capable of capturing loyalties and/or aversions to noninstitutionalized political parties that are brand new political organizations and in their early stages of development.

With this objective in mind, the survey measurement consists of a battery of three questions about voting intention on hypothetical elections in three-level public positions, not including the presidency, in order to avoid high levels of personalization (e.g. for Congress, Governor, and Mayor). One set of these three questions is included for each political party under study. The wording of the question is the following: *"Would you vote for a candidate of Party A for ...* (each of the following public positions)?" Based on a four-scale response (definitively, probably, probably not, and definitively not), first I label two types of partisanship according to the next rigorous patterns of answers. On the one hand, those respondents who answered that they would "definitively" vote for candidates of party A for each of the three positions asked are categorized as hardcore "positive partisans." On the other hand, those who responded that they would "definitively not" vote for candidates of party A for each of the same three positions are categorized as hardcore "negative partisans" or "anti-partisans." Other possible combinations (of "definitively" and "probably") in favor of candidates of party A can be labeled as "leaners," and combinations against candidates of party A can be labeled as soft anti-partisans. But for practical reasons, I propose to focus on the first two categories I have described (Table 1).

Table 1 Categorization of positive and negative partisanships according to survey answers to the question *Would you vote for a candidate of party A for ... ?*

Position	Definitively	Probably	Probably not	Definitively not
Congress	X			X
Governor	X			X
Mayor	X			X
Categories	(Hardcore) Positive partisan			(Hardcore) Negative partisan or anti-partisan

This is a very strict measurement of positive and negative partisanships. First, it avoids "softer" wordings (e.g. "closeness" or "sympathies" toward political parties) and better captures partisan loyalty and/or systematic partisan rejection. Second, inquiring for vote choice for multilevel positions has the intention to grasp fidelity toward a political party, rather than specific politicians. This is the reason why I recommend excluding presidential vote choice in the battery of questions. Finally, this "thicker" measurement permits us to capture partisan loyalty (or alternatively, partisan aversion) even though respondents do not recognize themselves publicly as "members" or "sympathizers." Partisanship – especially in post-partisan politics – is not necessarily a matter of membership or public militancy, but a demonstration of disciplined support in favor of a specific political organization.[2]

1.2 Typology

I propose to use set-theory in order to build a typology of four categories of (a)partisanships.[3] Based on the previous measurement, I define the membership of two basic groups. Those individuals who would definitively vote for candidates of any party belong to the set of positive partisans, while those who would definitively not vote for candidates of any party belong to the set of negative partisans. Based on the combinations of affiliations to these two sets, I develop a more complex picture of partisanships (positive, negative, and anti-establishment) and apartisanship. As it is evident, categories are not exclusive. I consider partisanship is a multidimensional phenomenon (Converse et al. 1969) since an individual can have multiple types of party IDs as explained in the next lines. This is one of the main differences between my classification and previous ones.

Individuals can hold positive and negative partisanship as long as their choices are coherent.[4] For example, in a bipartisan system, a person who is a partisan of party A can be, simultaneously, an anti-partisan of party B, and vice versa. Actually, this type of profile is what other authors consider "hardcore partisans" – individuals with strong identification with in-group and, at the same

---

[2] This innovative measurement, originally designed for capturing survival and emerging partisanships in Peru (Meléndez 2019), has been already successfully tested in different settings: non-institutionalized party systems like Venezuela and Colombia (Cyr & Meléndez 2016), institutionalized party systems like Chile (Meléndez & Rovira 2019), and European democracies (Melendez & Rovira 2021).

[3] An original version of this typology's construction can be found in Meléndez & Rovira 2019.

[4] Individuals who hold a positive partisanship and lack any negative partisanship are considered "positive partisans" according to Samuels and Zucco (2018) and "open partisans" according to Rose and Mishler (1998). According to the proposed typology, all individuals who definitively would vote for each of the three positions asked are labeled "positive partisans," independently of whether they hold negative partisanships or not.

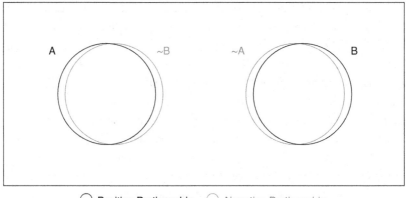

○ Positive Partisanship   ○ Negative Partisanship

Figure 4 Intersections between positive and negative partisanship

time, with strong antipathy for out-group (Samuels & Zucco 2018) – or "closed partisanship" – individuals for whom "party competition occurs in a world of Us versus Them, with both a positive and negative identification" (Rose & Mishler 1998, p. 223). However, the intersection of these two sets may vary. In some circumstances, the overlap is large, and most individuals who belong to the set of partisans of group A also belong to the set of anti-partisans of group B. This is the case of highly institutionalized party systems as displayed in Figure 4. But in other cases, the intersection is small and the group of those who hold negative partisanships and lack any positive partisanship ("pure anti-partisans" according to Samuels & Zucco 2018)[5] may be significantly larger than the overlap, as displayed in Figure 5. The difference is very important and as we will see in next sections, it is linked to low levels of PSI.

While it is illogical to hold two or more core positive partisanships, it is realistic that an individual can hold simultaneously two or more negative party IDs. It is very rare that an individual belongs simultaneously to two positive partisan groups,[6] but not if an individual belongs to two negative partisan groups, especially if the latter groups are comparatively larger than the positive ones and the intersection of negative partisan groups is considerable. For example, in a bipartisan system, independently from their positive

---

[5] Rose and Mishler (1998) label those individuals who have party animosities but without a positive party identification as "negative partisans." Samuels and Zucco (2018) call this group "negative partisans" as well, and alternatively "pure anti-partisans." I consider the latter a more accurate definition, since individuals who hold simultaneously a positive and negative partisanships should be recognized as negative identifiers.

[6] But it is not impossible if we consider positive political identification towards political movements that develops within a broader political party. For example: Kirchnerismo as a subset of Peronismo in Argentina. See Section 4.

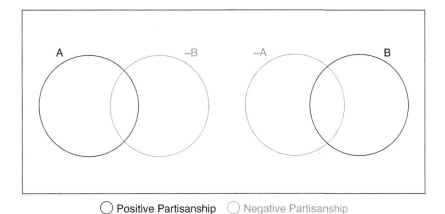

Figure 5 Intersections between positive and negative partisanship

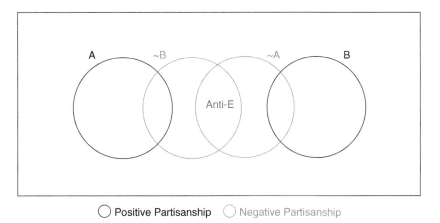

Figure 6 Intersections between positive and negative partisanship

partisanships, individuals may be regular anti-partisans (anti-party A or anti-party B) or, alternatively, they may hold both negative partisanships (anti-party A and anti-party B). The intersection of two or more sets of anti-partisans refers to the profile that I refer as "anti-establishment identifiers:" individuals who hold animosities toward the established political parties, as displayed in anti-E area in Figure 6.

Finally, we can identify a fourth group of individuals, those who do not belong to any of the preceding partisan or anti-partisan groups. I refer to them as apartisans, individuals who do not hold any positive or negative partisanship (and consequently cannot be categorized as anti-establishment identifiers). These individuals do not endorse any political party, but they do not reject

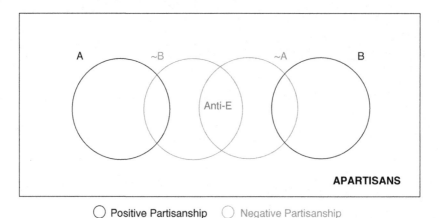

Positive Partisanship   Negative Partisanship

Figure 7 Intersections between positive and negative partisanship

partisan politics either, as indicated in Figure 7. Their absence of membership to the aforementioned groups speaks about their indifference to political parties, which have not been able to produce any likes or dislikes in them.

In general, taking apart conventional positive partisanship, I have proposed a typology that indicates three additional and different profiles of nonpositive partisans: negative identifiers (or anti-partisans), anti-establishment identifiers, and apartisans. I consider that this novel categorization is an advance based on previous efforts, and it covers the need to better understand a variety of settings characterized by partisan dealignment or by the decay of partisan politics.

1.3 Application of the Typology: Evidence from Chile and Brazil

Chile and Brazil are ideal settings to show the complete typology of post-partisan political identities.[7] The combination of relative stability of party competition (e.g. Mainwaring et al. 2018) and the emergence of anti-establishment attitudes (social unrest in Chile; rise of populist-rightist Jair Bolsonaro) can be translated at the individual level: those connected to political parties (positively or negatively), those who consistently reject the established parties, and those completely indifferent to the party system. I will argue that defining with precision the combination of these partisan and post-partisan political identities serves to better understand settings that combine probable party institutionalization processes with vigorous challenges to their respective establishments.

---

[7] A first application of this typology for the case of Chile was applied in Meléndez and Rovira 2019.

1.3.1 Chile

After the demise of the dictatorship, a two-partisan coalition was established with relatively success (e.g. Angell 2007). For the past thirty years, a center-left coalition (Concertación/Nueva Mayoría) and a center-right coalition (Alianza por Chile/Vamos Chile) have organized partisan politics in Chile. Based on this political control, colloquially labeled as "duopolio," the specialized literature has characterized Chilean party systems as stable, highly institutionalized (Mainwaring & Scully 1995), and based on programmatic linkages (e.g. Kitschelt et al. 2010; Levitsky & Roberts 2011). Social cleavages (Scully 1992; Valenzuela et al. 2007) and/or regimen preferences (Tironi & Agüero 1999; Torcal & Mainwaring 2003) had structured this party system before signals of dealignments emerged (Bargsted & Somma 2016).

The regularities of the electoral competition between these mainstream coalitions have created political identifications toward/against each of these parties' alliances, mostly organized around their respective ideological leanings. While individuals recognized themselves as sympathizers of specific political parties, they could also position themselves in favor or against each of these two political partnerships. In electoral terms, the Chilean party system of two coalitions had worked – at least before 2017 general elections[8] – as a bipartisan system, and it is reasonable to organize party identifications around them (Segovia 2009).

However, (positive) partisanships have declined consistently in the last decades. According to several survey research, identifications with the traditional political coalitions have decayed to proportions lower than 20 percent (CEP). According to Americas Barometer, Chile is, except for Guatemala, the Latin American country with the lowest level of individuals who identify themselves with political parties (Lupu 2015a). This evidence has added nuance to the conventional idea that Chilean party system is institutionalized. According to some authors, the Chilean party system had been "stable but uprooted" with loose connections with society (Altman & Luna 2011). Partisan disconnections, decreasing levels of electoral participation (e.g. Contreras & Navia 2013), and an increase in social unrest (e.g. Palacios & Ondetti 2018) have changed considerably the assessment of Chilean politics. Recent studies have announced a situation of political parties "under stress" (Morgan & Meléndez 2016) and a crisis of democratic representation (Luna 2016; Castiglioni & Rovira 2017). Actually, the unprecedented mobilization in October 2019 has made the menace of partisan establishment collapse something concrete (Somma et al. 2020).

---

[8] In 2017 elections, a third coalition, Frente Amplio, emerged as a competitive third force.

This apparent contradictory picture of Chilean politics (stable electoral competition at the party system level, all while parties remain disconnected from society) is better explained by employing the typology of post-partisan political identifications. If we just focus on the positive partisanship camp (supporters of the main two coalitions), we can detect, effectively, a decline in partisanship like the literature has shown (e.g. Lupu 2015a; Bargsted & Somma 2016). But if we also consider other types of political identifications, specifically post-partisan identities, we can understand at least three complementary phenomena: first, the contribution of negative partisanships to the relative stabilization of the party system; second, the real level of animosity toward the coalitional establishment ("duopolio"); and third, the spread of political disaffection.

Previous work – based on the proposed measurement and operationalization of partisanships – already shows the magnitude of these four partisanships in Chile in 2015 (Meléndez & Rovira 2019). Along with the specialized literature, the evidence demonstrates small shares of positive partisanships toward the traditional coalitions, a larger (and unconsidered by the literature) share of negative partisans, a significant intersection of negative partisanships (anti-establishment political identifiers), and a large set of apartisans (Figure 8).

Normally, the literature has conceived the non-(positive) partisan camp as homogenous or it has not been problematized adequately. The proposed typology applied to the Chilean case in 2015 allows us to describe three different profiles of individuals based on their partisans' affinities and rejections:

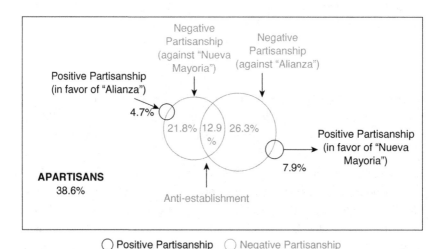

Figure 8 Different types of partisanship and their relative size in Chile 2015
Source: Meléndez & Rovira 2019

negative partisans (against Alianza, and against Nueva Mayoría), anti-establishment identifiers (anti-"duopolio"), and apartisans.

Negative partisans represent significant shares of the population and exceed their positive counterparts. 21.8 percent of respondents in a 2015 nationally representative survey qualified as anti-Nueva Mayoría, and 26.3 percent as anti-Alianza. Negative identifiers are not mere aversions toward specific party brands (coalition brands in this case). In order to be consistent and enduring, negative partisanships should be coalesced around ideological preferences and/or social identities, especially those that can produce an in-group/out-group positioning. As long as Chilean anti-partisanships (anti-Nueva Mayoría and anti-Alianza) achieve these requirements (political appeal and ideological self-positioning that articulates the negative partisanship of the memberships), they would contribute to the stability of the party system, solidifying political preferences. These are not in favor of political coalitions, but forcefully against them. Chilean party system stability cannot be explained by scant positive partisans, but rather by ample ideological and populist anti-partisans.

Anti-establishment identifiers reach 12.9 percent of the respondents. This is a more refined measurement of individuals who clearly rejected the "duopolio" in 2015. While conventional measurements calculate nonidentification with political parties at somewhere close to 85 percent (CEP 2019), the absence of party identification cannot be understood automatically as a rejection of the whole party system. The proposed typology is more precise in this regard and separates individuals who hold anti-establishment sentiments (12.9 percent) from those characterized by indifference (38.6 percent). Anti-establishment identifiers, those individuals who simultaneously reject both coalitions, should be coalesced also around ideological and/or political references. The opposition to the establishment can be interpreted by an ideological doctrine or by a populist discourse. In this sense, we would expect the animosity toward the Chilean "duopolio" to have a deeper sociological and/or political significance than the simple opposition to the regular politicians from the main two coalitions.

Finally, **apartisans** are the majority group in Chilean politics (38.6 percent) according to the configuration of partisanships displayed. Individuals categorized in this group lack any positive or negative partisanship. They express previously detected phenomena like voter alienation (e.g. Contreras & Navia 2013) and the fact that political parties have drifted away from civil society (Luna 2016). Ideological tenets cannot explain this group. Their political indifference is such that they reject any form of politicization, including populist approaches. Based on this, I consider that apartisanship better resembles political disaffection, which by 2015 was the predominant individual predisposition toward the Chilean political system.

Based on this evidence, it is reasonable to suggest that the relative stability of partisan competition in Chile until 2015 was based basically on the negative partisans rather than on the positive partisans that have maintained their identification (which the literature has described as in decay). At the same time, the existence of anti-establishment identifiers and indifferent apartisans speaks to the real magnitude of the social uprootedness of this presumably institutionalized party system. This description of individuals based on their party-IDs and post-partisan political identification is not particularly exclusive to the Chilean context. Original evidence from the Brazilian case shows a similar picture.

1.3.2 Brazil

The Brazilian party system – considered in the 1990s as an inchoate party system (Mainwaring & Scully 1995) – has relatively stabilized in recent years (Mainwaring et al. 2018). From 1994 to 2014, the Brazilian party system was institutionalized (Mainwaring et al. 2018), although for some authors this has been a process of party stabilization without institutionalization (Zucco 2015). In any case, the main actors of the party system have been stable over time, with notorious programmatic connections with society. PT on the left and MDB and PSDB on the center-right of the ideological spectrum have constituted the established political parties. In fact, PT and PSDB have established a regular duopoly in presidential elections, while legislative representation has remained fragmented.

The fate of PT has had significant impact on the party system stabilization in Brazil. Despite its party brand change, evidence has shown that many Brazilian citizens alternated between support to PT and independence without crossing party lines (Baker et al. 2016). In the long run, PT has been successful at cultivating mass partisanship identification based on their work with already organized civil society (Samules & Zucco 2014a), and its positive partisanship is very likely to endure independently from the support to Lula Da Silva, its historic leader (Samuels & Zucco 2014b). With its strong membership and organization, Brazilian politics have functioned around sympathies and antipathies regarding this political party. PT has developed a loyal partisanship but a strong anti-partisanship as well (Samuels & Zucco 2018). Part of the explanation of this "stabilization without roots" consists not only in the loyalties PT has nurtured but also in its rejection. Anti-petistas – individuals who oppose PT – might not belong to social organizations (might not have "roots" in society) – but vote according to their sentiments of repulsion to avoid PT's electoral victories.

By focusing on positive and negative partisans in Brazil, as Samuels and Zucco (2018) propose, it is possible to understand the apparently paradoxical situation of party "stabilization without roots."

Based on these three main political parties, I proceeded to empirically categorize Brazilians on this proposed political identification typology. In the case of Brazil, I measured three positive party identifications (PT, PSBD, and MDB), three negative partisanships (anti-PT, anti-PSDB, and anti-MDB), and consequently an anti-establishment political identity (those who hold simultaneously the aforementioned triple-negative partisanship), and apartisanship (those who lack any positive or negative party ID). Based on my original measurement, results show petismo as the most relevant positive partisanship (19.83 percent) and scant partisanships toward PSDB (2.9 percent) or MDB (2.4 percent), a significant simultaneous repulsion toward the three mainstream parties (23.8 percent), a significant share of negative identifiers (43.8 percent as anti-PT, 56.8 percent as anti-PSDB, and 61.8 percent as anti-MDB), and a significant sector of Brazilians who qualify as apartisans (17.7 percent). The corresponding information is displayed in Figure 9.

Like Chile, the proposed typology is useful to explain different types of connections between individuals and political parties. Positive partisanships toward established parties and their negative counterparts tend to coalesce around ideological considerations (e.g. Samuels & Zucco 2018). Although positive partisans (especially those related to PSDB and MDB) correspond to

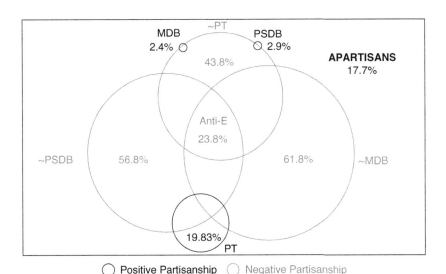

Figure 9 Different types of partisanship and their relative size in Brazil 2018
Source: Ipsos 2018

a quarter of the population (25.1 percent qualifies as core followers of PT, PSDB, and MDB), ideological connections are prevalent due to the sizable population of negative identifiers. The predominance of programmatic political linkages between anti-partisans and the electoral supply has contributed to the perceived path toward institutionalization that the specialized literature has reported as a sole consequence of the predominance of PT. However, its stability is mostly explained by negative partisanships, rather than by PT's following.

Anti-establishment identifiers formed a third group composed by the intersection of the corresponding three negative partisanships. 23.8 percent of the population holds anti-PT, anti-PSDB, and anti-MDB negative identifications, which represents a solid opposition to the traditional establishment. This measurement was provided before the 2018 electoral campaign, but there are reasons to argue that support for Jair Bolsonaro was cultivated among anti-establishment identifiers (Fuks et al. 2021). The election of Bolsonaro cannot be explained exclusively by resentment toward the PT, but also due to a more general rejection of the cultural values of the political establishment (Rennó 2020).

Finally, there is a fourth group composed by apartisans, individuals who do not hold any positive or negative partisanship. According to previous research, a significant proportion of Brazilians might fall in this category, which is mobilized by "pork and pageantry" (Samuels & Zucco 2018, p. 7). According to the proposed measurement, 17.7 percent of Brazilians in 2018 qualified as apartisans, a percentage that is lower than detected by previous research.[9] Although some studies have tackled this group of the population, there is no convincing evidence about its political and ideological characteristics, besides their political apathy. Overall, the Brazilian party system has developed certain levels of stability mainly due to the combination of positive and negative partisanships. Negative partisans are the most salient group, and apartisans are fewer than expected, according to the results of previous research.

In summary, Chilean and Brazilian party systems have been described as stable but normally uprooted (except for PT in Brazil). Although positive partisanships are weak in these countries, the specialized literature has emphasized the apparent pro-institutionalization as the force behind this stability. If we just focus on the traditional positive partisanships, we end up describing a potential paradox: stability without social roots. By incorporating post-partisan political identities, it is feasible to go deeper in this analysis. It is

---

[9] According to Samuels and Zucco (2018), non-partisans have fluctuated between 29.44 percent in 201 to 45.61 percent in 2014, percentages considerably higher than reported by my research. The difference is due to the exclusion in Samuel's and Zucco's measurements of anti-PSDB and anti-MDB among the negative partisans.

reasonable to say that in both cases, negative partisanships have collaborated to stabilize the party system. Although negative partisanships are not socially rooted through intermediate social organizations (social protests in Chile do not respond to the leaders of traditional parties; anti-petista movements in Brazil have not institutionalized), they explain electoral choices and political behavior in general. Anti-partisans behave in predictable ideological ways, which have collaborated with the programmatic differentiation among elites that has helped preserve this system from the fate of party-system collapses (Mainwaring et al. 2018).

Larger shares of the population in anti-partisan sets are not necessarily a positive sign for PSI. Negative partisans can be coalesced around ideological tenets but also around populist appeals. The relevance of populist sentiments increases in specific profiles of negative partisans: anti-establishment identifiers (Meléndez & Rovira 2019). Those individuals who simultaneously reject the mainstream parties constitute the demand for the emergence of populist anti-establishment leaders. While in 2015 in Chile, anti-establishment identifiers grouped 12.9 percent of the population, in 2018 in Brazil they totaled 23.8 percent. While Chileans had continued endorsing mainstream presidential candidates (Piñera was elected in the 2017 elections, but a mainstream candidate was not elected in 2021), Brazilians crossed the line and elected a right-wing populist politician like Jair Bolsonaro. The previous size of the anti-establishment camp could work as an announcement of acute social protests against the establishment (in Chile) and of the potential success of disruptive forces (in Brazil).

Surprisingly, apartisanship could be understood as a dike toward populism. Both in Chile and Brazil, apartisans are indifferent to political parties, which include populist projects. Their political indifference is so strong that they repel any type of politicization, including populist versions. While in Chile, apartisans remained (at least until 2015) at a third of the population, in Brazil, apartisans are a reduced sector. Apartisanship should be understood not as a neutral force, but as a barrier impeding the emergence of populist projects. This is a completely different role that the literature has not yet detected, and that I will develop in the next sections.

So far, I have applied the proposed typology to two different settings, considering their similar levels of PSI. In the next sections, I will explore more deeply the characteristics of each of these post-partisan identifications in different Latin American countries in order to demonstrate the particular usefulness of each category to explain arenas of post-party system collapse (negative partisanship in Peru) and challenges to PSI (anti-establishment identities and apartisanship in Honduras, Argentina, Brazil, and Chile).

2 Negative Partisanship

In May 2009, the future winner of the Nobel Prize in Literature and Peruvian political factotum Mario Vargas Llosa declared in a journalistic interview: "I don't believe that my fellow countrymen are so silly as to push us to choose between AIDS and terminal cancer a dilemma represented by a hypothetical runoff between Ollanta Humala and Keiko Fujimori." Two years after that statement, the presidential runoff in Peru confirmed Vargas Llosa's worst nightmare. Under this extreme scenario, Vargas Llosa decided to endorse Humala because he considered him as the lesser of two evils. In his sole attempt to get elected as President of Peru in 1990, Vargas Llosa was defeated by Alberto Fujimori, Keiko's father and founding leader of fujimorismo. Since then, the writer has retired from electoral and partisan politics but has been a permanent opponent to the Fujimoris and a critic of their legacy. Vargas Llosa could broker agreements with former political rivals like Alan García, but he has never been indifferent to fujimorismo. In reality, until 2021 presidential elections, we can consider Vargas Llosa to be the perfect anti-fujimorista.

The aversion that Vargas Llosa held toward fujimorismo was blocked by another negative partisanship: anti-communism. In 2021 presidential elections, the Nobel Prize surprised Peruvians by endorsing Keiko Fujimori in the ballotage against radical left-wing populist Pedro Castillo. Only a more profound political repudiation (anti-communism) neutralized Vargas Llosa's opposition toward fujimorismo. However, not many anti-fujimoristas followed the writer's conversion. Actually, millions of Peruvians repudiate this political sector. And we can argue that anti-fujimorismo is one of the most prevalent negative partisanships in Peru currently, not the only one. Since the mid-twentieth century, political alignments in Peru cannot be explained without any reference to the division between aprismo/anti-aprismo (Manrique 2009). This political cleavage has remained, with ups and downs, relevant in the public sphere even until the present day, when Alianza Popular Revolucionaria Americana (APRA) has become a minor political party. The 2021 elections brought back another negative partisanship: anti-communism, an enduring but latent animadversion toward revolutionary projects, through military reforms (Velasco Alvarado's dictatorship) or as a violent insurgency (Shining Path). The political rise of a populist leader, Pedro Castillo, via a Marxist-Leninist political party (Perú Libre), made more salient this negative partisanship that is frequent in other Latin American countries, as well. It is fair to say that in order to understand Peruvian politics, it is more important to track anti-fujimorismo, anti-aprismo, and anti-communism than any other positive party identification.

The relevance of negative partisanship in Peru is not an exception. In Argentina, since the coup *d'etat* that overthrew Juan Domingo Perón in 1955, most of the remainder of the Argentinian twentieth century was explained by the division of peronismo/anti-peronismo (Nállim 2014), a divide that has survived. In the twenty-first century, a new version of this separation is represented by kirchnerismo (the political movement that dominates the Peronismo nowadays, established by the rule of Nestor Kirchner and Cristina Fernández de Kirchner) and anti-kirchnerismo (the political opponents to the power of the Kirchners). This political cleavage has been called "The Crack" (*La Grieta*) to express the profound political, cultural, and sociological division between these two camps, that in specific acute junctures polarizes Argentinians.

In other Latin American countries, we can find similar phenomena. Opposition to certain political parties or political movements has gained autonomy and relevance. Independent from political parties, and in most cases, exceeding these organizations, negative partisanships have emerged in Brazil (anti-PT), Venezuela (anti-chavismo), Colombia (anti-uribismo), and other countries. Against political parties or nascent political movements, millions of active and informed citizens have mobilized against the political parties they hate, although they are not willing to maintain loyalty to the opportunistic vehicles that circumstantially express their fury. Negative identifiers have become protagonists of current politics, but few researchers have studied them comparatively in Latin America.

This section is the most extensive attempt to cover this gap. Following the methodological considerations explained in previous sections, I have applied my original measurement of positive and negative partisanship and adapted it to different party-system configurations, considering different types of political organizations: political parties (e.g. PT in Brazil), political coalitions (e.g. Nueva Mayoría and Chile Vamos in Chile), and political movements not necessarily organized in political parties (e.g. fujimorismo in Peru, uribismo in Colombia, kirchnerismo in Argentina). Measurements of the main positive and (their respective) negative partisanships are considered for comparative reasons. In all cases, nationally representative face-to-face surveys were conducted by prestigious pollsters.

Fewer individuals in new democracies hold positive party identifications (Dalton & Weldon 2007), while more individuals hold negative partisanships. My research shows that more Latin Americans tend to develop negative partisanships than positive partisanships. Evidence displays that, in agreement with the literature, positive partisanships represent small shares of the population. In the cases where it was possible to study more than one point in time – Mexico 2018 and 2019, Peru 2011, 2016, and 2019 – assessed positive partisanships have declined (with the exception of Movimiento Regeneración Nacional (MORENA) in Mexico, which has been stable). On the other hand, the corresponding negative partisanships are more relevant numerically. In almost every case (again the exception is MORENA in Mexico), individuals who hold negative partisanships exceed their counterparts' positive identifiers. In general, in terms of the size of their share, negative partisanships are more significant. Political parties with proportionally small sets of followers tend to produce larger sets of anti-partisans – in most cases more than half of the populations. In Brazil, PSDB accounts for 2.9 percent of partisans but 56.8 percent of anti-partisans; similarly, MDB accounts for 2.39 percent of partisans and 61.87 percent of anti-partisans. In Peru, APRA in 2011 accounted for only 2.9 percent of partisans but 56 percent of anti-partisans. Although its positive partisanships had slightly increased up to 4.9 percent by 2016 and 5.2 percent by 2019, the corresponding anti-partisanships increased more significantly, up to 66.5 percent and 60.6 percent, respectively. In Mexico, Partido Revolucionario Institucional (PRI) shows a similar dynamic. In 2018, 8.61 percent of individuals were categorized as priistas, a percentage that then declined to 2.8 percent the next year. Anti-priismo, on the other hand, increased from 40.6 percent to 49.6 percent, respectively (Table 2). Old and discredited political parties have survived and maintained small (positive) partisanships, but, at the same time, have created the largest anti-partisanships in the continent.

2.1 What are Negative Partisans Made Of?

Positive and negative partisanships, conceived as long-standing psychological attachments, are not ephemeral adscriptions. In order to be enduring, political identifications need to be based on ideological tenets (such as programmatic preferences) or to ensure social identity ingredients (such as feelings of group memberships) (Greene 2004). Like positive partisanships, negative partisanships are made of rational considerations as well as affective connections toward specific political parties (Bankert 2021). Both dimensions can help shape an amalgam of ideological and sentimental opposition to groups that individuals consider that they do not belong to or, even, that they reject. Anti-peronistas in Argentina or anti-petistas in Brazil do reject peronismo and PT, respectively, not only because they perceive themselves far from those parties in the ideological continuum, but also because they might see followers of these parties as socially distant. For example, anti-peronistas normally perceive themselves as belonging to the upper echelons of Argentinian society, characterized by the "well behaved," restraint, and proper manners, while peronistas tend to belong to less sophisticated sectors associated with populist appeals (Ostiguy 2009).

Table 2 Measures of main positive and negative partisanships in Latin America

Country and year	Positive partisanship	Percentage	Negative partisanship	Percentage
Argentina 2019	Peronismo	25.11	Anti-peronismo	21.42
	Kircherismo	21.89	Anti-kirchnerismo	42.80
	PRO	13.46	Anti-PRO	46.52
Brazil 2018	PT	19.83	Anti-PT	43.79
	PSDB	2.96	Anti-PSDB	56.88
	MDB	2.39	Anti-MDB	61.87
Chile 2015	Nueva Mayoría	9.05	Anti-Nueva Mayoría	28.85
	Chile Vamos	5.66	Anti-Chile Vamos	33.89
Colombia 2019	Uribismo	6.89	Anti-uribismo	35.66
Honduras 2018	Nacional	24.18	Anti-nacionalismo	32.10
	Liberal	9.74	Anti-liberalismo	30.90
	LIBRE	13.71	Anti-LIBRE	38.59
Mexico 2018	PRI	8.61	Anti-PRI	40.68
	PAN	8.55	Anti-PAN	31.16
	MORENA	23.64	Anti-MORENA	18.59
Mexico 2019	PRI	2.82	Anti-PRI	49.67
	PAN	4.75	Anti-PAN	46.45

Table 2 (cont.)

Country and year	Positive partisanship	Percentage	Negative partisanship	Percentage
	MORENA	24.31	Anti-MORENA	7.30
Peru 2011	APRA	2.91	Anti-APRA	56.51
	Fujimorismo	10.05	Anti-fujimorismo	39.55
Peru 2016	APRA	4.92	Anti-APRA	54.19
	Fujimorismo	9.80	Anti-fujimorismo	34.90
Peru 2019	APRA	5.27	Anti-APRA	66.51
	Fujimorismo	8.78	Anti-fujimorismo	60.69

Source: Isonomía Consultores in Argentina, Ipsos in Brazil, UDP in Chile, LAPOP in Colombia, Borge & Asociados in Honduras, Parametría in Mexico, and IOP-PUCP and Ipsos in Peru.

In order to tackle these two possible dimensions (ideological and sociological) that might glue negative partisanship, I consider conventional ideological self-perception and populist "thin-ideological" appeals as variables statistically associated with negative partisanships. Regarding the former, as long as ideology is a bipolar cognitive tool (Medeiros & Noel 2013), it is very likely to have an effect on explaining positive and negative partisans. In this research, I have used a traditional self-positioning scale from 1 to 10 in order to ask individuals about their programmatic preferences. Regarding the latter, in most of the studied countries, a "thin" populist ideology index has been also included: An index of six items that captures populist attitudes corresponding to a Maniquean division of society and conceptions of popular sovereignty (Hawkins et al. 2012). As a moral conceptualization, populism can work as another "ideological" coalescing factor that divides and polarizes society. I hypothesize that programmatic preferences and populist attitudes can be the glue of negative partisans in most Latin American countries.[10]

After performing logistical regression models for every positive and negative partisanship included in the study, I corroborate that ideological self-positioning successfully articulates many party identifications in the expected direction.[11] Regarding positive partisanships and controlling for the aforementioned sociodemographics, ideological self-positioning[12] statistically explains the articulation of peronismo/kirchnerismo and Propuesta Republicana (PRO) (left-wing and right-wing, respectively) in Argentina, PT, PSDB, and MDB (left-wing in the first case and right-wing in the latter two) in Brazil, Nueva Mayoría's and Chile Vamos's followings (left-wing and right-wing, respectively), uribismo (right-wing) in Colombia, hardcore followers of Partido Nacional, Partido Liberal, and Partido Libertad y Refundación

---

[10] Sociodemographic variables, depending on idiosyncratic considerations, might have an effect as complementary articulators of these identities. Class and geographical residence might be relevant in contexts of national polarization. Respondents' income and region have been included as the respective proxies. Education (measured in years of schooling), Gender, and Age have been also considered as control variables.

[11] I ran logistical models considering every positive and negative partisanships as dichotomic dependent variables. I consider conventional self-positioning 1–10 scale (1 = extreme left; 10 = extreme right) as a proxy for ideology, and a 6-item index on populist appeals as the main independent variables. All models control for income, age, gender (1 = male), education, and zone (1 = urban; 0 = rural; in Argentina: 1 = Gran Buenos Aires; 0 = rest of the country). Populist index was not included in Peru 2011 and Peru 2016. "Zone" variables were not included in Mexico and Peru 2011 and Peru 2016. For more details, see Annex 1.

[12] The conventional ideological self-positioning scale question has advantages and disadvantages. It has been extensively employed in public opinion researchers and it is very useful for comparative purposes. However, its utility is constraint on contextual factors (Zechmeister & Corral 2013) and item response rate is not high in some countries. Being aware of these limitations, I proceeded to employ this item as an available proxy for capturing ideological preferences.

(LIBRE) (right-wing in the first case and left-wing in the latter two) in Honduras, PRI and PAN (right-wingers in both cases) in Mexico (in 2018 and 2019), and APRA and fujimorismo (both right-wingers) in Peru in 2011 and 2019. In most cases, statistical relationships are significant at the 99 percent confidence interval.

Exceptions are few and might be explained by circumstantial factors. Hardcore partisans of MORENA in Mexico are not influenced by ideological self-positioning, probably due to the catch-all proselytism of its leader López Obrador. Fujimoristas and apristas, in Peru in 2016, are not coalesced either around ideological considerations. Although there is evidence regarding the right-wing ideological glue of fujimoristas and apristas in 2011 and 2019, during the 2016 electoral campaign, ideological considerations were more effective mobilizing anti-partisans rather than positive partisans. In general, ideological considerations have exerted influence over organizing positive partisans in Latin America, in different party institutionalization settings. The partial exception is Peru, precisely the weakest party system of the cases studied.

Similar ingredients compose negative partisanships. Ideological self-positioning works as an effective cohesive element of anti-peronismo/anti-kirchnerismo and anti-PRO (right-wing and left-wing, respectively) in Argentina, anti-petismo, anti-PSDB, and anti-MDB (right-wing in the first case, left-wing in the latter two) in Brazil, anti-Nueva Mayoría and anti-Chile Vamos (right-wing and left-wing, respectively) in Chile, left-wing anti-uribismo in Colombia, anti-nacionalismo, anti-liberalismo, and anti-LIBRE (left-wing in the first case, right-wing in the latter two) in Honduras, anti-PRI and anti-PAN (left-wing in both cases), and anti-MORENA (right-wing) in Mexico 2018, and anti-fujimorismo and anti-aprismo (left-wing in both cases) in Peru in 2011, 2016, and 2019. The only exceptions of cases of negative partisanships that are not statically explained by ideological considerations are the Mexicans' anti-partisanships in 2019. Overall, it is reasonable to state that negative partisanships in Latin America have a notorious ideological component.

In most countries where I included survey measurement of populist attitudes, this Manichean worldview also plays an amalgamating role in the shaping of negative partisanships. With the exception of anti-peronismo and anti-PRO's identification in Argentina, anti-liberalismo partisanship in Honduras, anti-PRI and anti-PAN in Mexico in 2019, populist attitudes tend to be associated with the cohesiveness of anti-partisanship. Rejection of specific political parties (especially if those are associated with the political establishment) fosters populist sentiments. Considering only logistic models with 95 percent and 99 percent confidence intervals, populist sentiments are coalescing factors behind anti-petismo, anti-PSDB, and anti-MDB in Brazil, anti-Nueva Mayoría and anti-Chile Vamos in Chile, anti-uribismo in Colombia, anti-nacionalismo in Honduras, anti-PRI and anti-PAN in Mexico (2018), and anti-aprismo and anti-fujimorismo in Peru (2019). As expected, attraction to populist appeals does not play a significant role in coalescing positive partisanship with the exceptions of uribismo in Colombia, and MORENA in Mexico in 2019. Populist worldviews turn out a complementary ideological glue that reinforces conventional programmatic preferences in order to structure negative partisanships in Latin America. Negative partisans have their own ideological preferences (left-wing or right-wing), but they share this feeling of repulsion to the establishment and the need to be associated with idealized "people" in contraposition to the elites.

In some countries, sociodemographic divides contribute to the cohesiveness of positive and negative partisanships, especially class division. In Argentina, while peronismo, kirchnerismo, and anti-PRO are prevalent among lower classes, anti-peronismo, anti-kirchnerismo, and PRO's hardcore are associated with higher incomes. In Brazil, while petismo (and anti-PSDB and anti-MDB) is negatively associated with income, anti-petismo is positively associated. Some political identities are also shaped by age. In Argentina, PRO's hardcore following and anti-kirchnerismo are positively associated with age. In Chile, the established political coalitions (Nueva Mayoría and Chile Vamos) are more prevalent among older cohorts. In Mexico, the traditional PRI has better stakes in older individuals. In Peru, consistently across three points in time, the propensity of being anti-fujimorista or anti-aprista increases with age.

Overall, negative partisans are basically coalesced by programmatic preferences and populist appeals. From left to right, part of the perceived hatred they apparently hold is based on the Manichean worldview they share, in which they conceive themselves as members of an anti-establishment camp, a sort of in-group identification defined by the opposition to the "elitist" political parties they reject. In some cases, class divisions and age determinants enforce these identifications. Negative partisans tend to develop populist sentiments except when an anti-establishment political party emerges. Among the cases studied, MORENA in Mexico is notorious because populist attitudes solidified its positive partisanship. However, these populist and ideological negative partisans have not necessarily converted their cohesiveness into a positive partisanship and consequently have maintained themselves disentangled from the establishment. Negative partisans are not necessarily capable of developing positive partisanships associated with the decaying or emerging establishment since they tend to reproduce populist preferences.

2.2 Peru: A Democracy with Negative Partisans

Negative partisanships have existed in institutionalized and noninstitutionalized party systems. In the previous section, I presented a comparative measurement of negative partisanships across several Latin American countries and different party-system settings. Although measuring negative partisanship has recently received more attention from comparativists, negative partisans have always existed. However, there are some contexts in which negative partisanships are predominant and more independent from positive partisanships, especially the most relevant party identifications. This is the case of Peru and its historic difficulty to mount a party system.

Partisanship, positive or negative, is defined as an "unmoved mover" that slowly changes in time (Fiorina 1981). Accordingly, it is apt to analyze its evolution in a specific national arena through a considerable period of time. Due to the originality of the measurement proposed in this Element, it is not possible to trace the progression of partisanship through long periods. For this reason, I have prioritized a cross-national comparison instead of a longitudinal one. However, in the particular case of Peru, I have applied the same original measurement in three different moments (2011, 2016, and 2019) with minor variations.

Peru is an ideal case to study the predominance of anti-partisanships. Historically, we can trace two politically powerful negative partisanships – anti-aprismo and anti-fujimorismo – that independently from ephemeral political parties have endured through times. Regarding the first one, the Peruvian twentieth century can be characterized as a struggle between anti-oligarchic APRA's push to access power via elections, and anti-aprista coalitions (the military and the conservative elites, mainly) to stop it. Although Peruvians were not able to construct a solid party system during the past century (Tanaka 1998), the aprista/anti-aprista political division considerably organized the political arena. Despite the importance of this political cleavage, this topic was understudied by the social sciences. Once APRA finally accessed power and entered the political establishment at the end of the past century, a renewed establishment/anti-establishment division emerged with the surprising appearance of fujimorismo.

Anti-fujimorismo is the most relevant negative partisanship in contemporary Peru. In order to understand its complexity, we need to go back to the 1990s. Alberto Fujimori arose as an anti-establishment outsider in the 1990 presidential elections, and against all odds defeated pro-establishment outsider Mario Vargas Llosa, who ran in alliance with the traditional right-wing parties (Grompone & Degregori 1990). Once in office, Fujimori constructed a competitive authoritarian regime with clientelistic and "law and order" policies that cemented his popular support (Cotler & Grompone 2000). Although he had access to state resources during his ten-year administration, he did not invest in party-building or partisanship promotion (Murakami 2007). He did not sponsor a "party brand" and instead of promoting militants for his volatile electoral vehicles (Cambio 90, Nueva Mayoría, Vamos Vecino), he encouraged his followers to label themselves as "independents." Involuntarily, he was nurturing in his own following, a nascent partisanship without a party organization (Meléndez 2019).

In 2000, Alberto Fujimori abandoned office due to corruption scandals and exiled himself to Japan, while the Peruvian justice charged him for crimes committed during his tenure and under his responsibility (Murakami 2007). The collapse of his government knocked down his popularity and legacy and created opportunities for his opponents. As a result, few people would publicly recognize their loyalties toward fujimorismo. Some scholars even believed that fujimorismo had disappeared by the beginning of the twenty-first century (e.g. Carrión 2006). In order to return to active politics in Peru and to face trial under better political conditions, Fujimori reorganized his cadres and put together a new electoral vehicle, called Alianza para el Futuro, for the 2006 general elections. Martha Chávez, a former speaker of Congress, was the chosen presidential candidate, and Fujimori's daughter and former First Lady Keiko Fujimori was the head of the Legislative list in Lima. Surprisingly, 7 percent of the electorate voted for fujimorismo, who obtained 13 seats (of 120) in the new Parliament.

Since the 2006 electoral campaign, the chances of fujimorismo returning to power increased. Although Alberto Fujimori was jailed and sentenced to twenty-five years, Keiko Fujimori turned out to be very competitive in electoral politics. Fujimorismo under her leadership rearranged their political resources and initiated what they called an "institutionalization path." Although they did not win the presidential elections in 2011, 2016 or 2021, Fuerza Popular – the new fujimorista party label – got an unprecedented parliamentary majority in 2016 (73 of 130 seats). In fact, one of the reasons why fujimorismo could not accomplish its objectives was the solid anti-fujimorista coalitions that had articulated to avoid a return of fujimorismo to power.

Anti-fujimorismo is not embodied in any formal political organization. There is no such thing as an anti-fujimorista political party. It is a coalition of small but active social organizations (most of them originated in the Human Rights movement) ideologically inclined to the left. The corresponding anti-partisanship exceeds the mobilization capacity and memberships of these groups. Anti-fujimorismo, as a political identity, exists independently of presidential candidates that try to circumstantially appeal to critics of fujimorismo or independently of active social leaders. While fujimorismo should be understood as a nascent partisanship based on a weak institutionalized organization, anti-fujimorismo should be understood as a negative partisanship independent from any political organization. A fragile party system with weak political organizations does not prevent the shaping of partisanships and anti-partisanships like fujimorismo and anti-fujimorismo.

Fujimorismo/anti-fujimorismo has, then, emerged as a profound political divide in Peru. While the political division aprismo/anti-aprismo that originated in the past century has lost leverage – especially due to the loss of competitiveness of aprista candidacies – the fujimorismo/anti-fujimorismo has organized the Peruvian system lately. Accordingly, the electoral triumphs of Ollanta Humala (2011), Pedro Pablo Kuczynski (2016), and Pedro Castillo (2021) over Keiko Fujimori (in all of these elections) can be interpreted as victories of anti-fujimorismo. In order to explain the consistency of persistent anti-aprismo and solid anti-fujimorismo, in comparison to their positive counterparts and their relevance, I proceed to show survey opinion evidence of the main positive and negative partisanships prevalent in contemporary Peruvian politics.

Evidence shows a relative stability of positive and negative partisanship in the nine-year period of study. First, hardcore partisans of the two more persistent political parties that prevail in Peruvian politics – APRA and Fuerza Popular, the current fujimorista organization – represent relatively small shares of the population. Based on my proposed measurement, aprista loyalties totaled 2.9 percent in 2011, 4.9 percent in 2016, and 5.3 percent in 2019. Hardcore fujimoristas represented 10.1 percent in 2011, 9.8 percent in 2016, and 8.8 percent in 2019. While other political parties' sympathizers have varied considerably and even disappeared, apristas and fujimoristas have kept loyalties constant, a good evidence of partisanship.[13] In one of the most deinstitutionalized party systems of the continent (Mainwaring et al. 2018), it is expected that positive partisans are marginal but steady. No other political party has registered a solid following throughout this decade.

In contrast, most Peruvians qualify as negative partisans. Negative partisanships have attracted larger shares of the population in a persistent manner. Based on my proposed measurement, anti-aprismo reached 56.5 percent in 2011,

---

[13] In 2011, I included the proposed measurement of partisanship for Partido Nacionalista Peruano, obtaining 4.1 percent of core followers. By the next survey, in 2016, less than 1 percent of respondents considered themselves as "nacionalistas." Respondents who sympathize with Peruanos por el Kambio (PPK), Partido Solidaridad Nacional (PSN), Frente Amplio (FA), Acción Popular (AP) were included in Figures 10, 11, and 12 (circles in dotted lines). In these cases, the measurements correspond to the conventional question "With which political party do you sympathize?"

54.1 percent in 2016, and 66.5 percent in 2019. In the case of anti-fujimorismo, the corresponding percentages were 39.6 percent in 2011, 34.9 percent in 2016, and 60.7 percent in 2019. The notorious increase in the last measurement, in both cases, might be related to the acute political crisis triggered by the Lava Jato scandal in 2018. Testimonies from Brazilian construction officials (*Odebrecht*, OAS, and *Camargo Correa*) accused many high-ranking politicians of different political organizations of being accomplices. However, fujimoristas and apristas were the most discredited. Judicial authorities employing preventive imprisonment jailed twice-presidential candidate Keiko Fujimori, the president of Fuerza Popular. They also attempted to proceed similarly with former president Alan García, the historic leader of APRA, but he committed suicide to avoid incarceration. Meanwhile, tensions between the Executive and Legislative ended up with the dissolution of the latter, which was at that point under fujimorista control. The association of apristas and fujimoristas with corruption scandals and the imprisonment and disappearance of their respective leaders made these negative partisanships even more deep and expansive.

Negative partisanships are central to Peruvian politics. While political sympathies are volatile, negative partisans are the axis of political alignments. Ephemeral political parties have tried to capitalize the negative partisanship camp. In the 2011 elections, Partido Nacionalista Peruano (PNP) attempted to cultivate its own following based on the opposition to fujimorismo and aprismo. Most of the 4.1 percent of PNP's sympathizers qualified as anti-fujimoristas

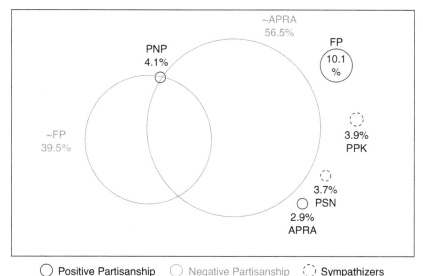

Figure 10 Different types of partisanship and their relative size in Peru 2011

and/or anti-apristas (Figure 10). Nacionalista leader Ollanta Humala won the presidential election, but he was not able to transform this electoral support into a solid following. By the next presidential elections, in 2016, nacionalistas practically disappeared. However, the anti-fujimorista and anti-aprista camp was still politically attractive. This time, Pedro Pablo Kuczynski successfully appealed to that space. While in 2011, Peruanos Por el Kambio (PPK)'s followers (3.9 percent) were not aligned in the anti-fujimorista and anti-aprista spectrum, five years later more than half of PPK's sympathizers (24.7 percent of the total population) qualified as anti-fujimoristas and/or anti-apristas (Figure 11). Other political parties like Frente Amplio (FA) and Acción Popular (AP) also attempted to capitalize this space, but they were not as successful as PPK.

However, the anti-fujimorista and anti-aprista camp does not have a political owner. After the 2018 political crisis, PPK's political capital was reduced to a minimum. Only 6.6 percent of respondents declared themselves as sympathizers of this political organization, and they marginally occupied this double-"anti" camp (Figure 12). The PPK's debacle is explained by the resignation of Pedro Pablo Kuczynski to the presidency in 2018, which was also due to corruption investigations. He has been under house arrest since 2019. The loss of prestige drove some remaining representatives of the political organization to change PPK's label to "Contigo." This party's list of candidates for Congress in 2020 failed to obtain 1 percent of valid votes. Other minor political parties like AP have tried to appeal to negative partisans, but they have not been successful (yet).

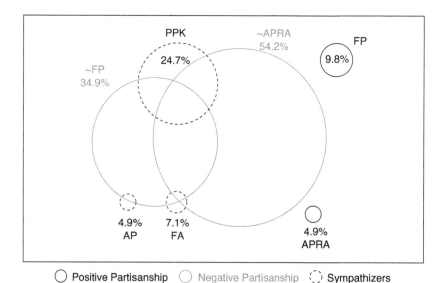

Figure 11 Different types of partisanship and their relative size in Peru 2016

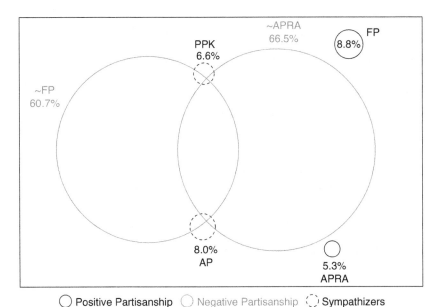

○ Positive Partisanship ○ Negative Partisanship ⦙ Sympathizers

Figure 12 Different types of partisanship and their relative size in Peru 2019

As it has been explained, in a context of fluid political parties, negative partisanships are essential to understand political links among Peruvians.

The enduring and persistent proportions of anti-partisans in Peru are explained by their ideological cohesiveness (Table 2). In terms of programmatic preferences, both anti-aprismo and anti-fujimorismo tend to lean to left-wing positions. Although these negative partisans do not belong to any political organization, they share a common ideological preference toward the left. Additionally, they are coalesced by a "thin" ideology–like populism. It is not a coincidence in a context of a political establishment in crisis (like in 2019) that populist appeals statistically explain both negative partisanships at the 99 percent confidence interval, controlled by sociodemographics (see Annex 1). And finally, Peruvian negative partisanships are also related to age. In all logistical models performed with survey data of 2011, 2016, and 2019, respondents' age is positively associated with anti-aprismo and anti-fujimorismo. While other sociodemographic variables play a partial explanatory role (e.g. in some models, anti-fujimorismo is more prevalent among men), age is definitively associated with both negative partisans. Thus, anti-partisanships in Peru have activated and mobilized the historical memory of the elderly population, which explains part of their success in impeding the return of fujimorismo to office.

The hegemonic dynamics of picking the "lesser of two evils" ("mal menor") in Peru have not contributed to the forging of new and socially rooted political parties. Most Peruvians have developed antipathies toward two specific political parties (APRA and fujimorismo) and have voted, at least in 2011, 2016, and 2021 elections, in order to prevent these parties from getting to office. Despite this, they have not developed any positive preferences in favor of these parties' contenders. Peru has been infertile ground for developing political parties and for forging positive partisans. Aprista and fujimorista partisans are, actually, the exception. But Peru is a fecund arena for negative partisanships like anti-apristas and anti-fujimoristas. The predominant literature has characterized Peruvian politics as a "democracy without parties" (Tanaka 2005), but a more accurate assessment is to characterize it as a democracy with negative partisans.

3 Anti-establishment Identifiers and Apartisans

Specialists have explained the reasons and the processes that lead individuals to abandon party identifications in Latin America, in settings characterized by dramatic transformations of the partisan landscapes (e.g. Lupu 2015a). When political parties dilute their brands, by ideological inconsistencies and/or programmatic convergence, individuals who used to recognize themselves with social stereotypes associated to these political parties no longer perceive themselves as part of these groups (Lupu 2015b). Moreover, extreme reasons – like economic and social crises – imply that most people in a specific political arena take the decision to abandon established positive partisanships at the same time, provoking a party-system collapse (Morgan 2011). Economic crises or corruption scandals can trigger processes of systematic decline in party identification (Seawright 2012).

Under serious problems of high-level corruption or disastrous economic performance, citizens can feel unprecedented heights of anxiety or fury. According to Seawright (2012), anger is the most probable reaction when facing these kinds of situations, since this type of emotion is normally associated with risk-accepting behaviors like voting for outsiders. In his work on party-system collapse, the author indicates how anger caused by systemic political corruption contributes to the simultaneous erosion of positive identifications associated with the established traditional parties. Anger is the psychological base for a systematic abandonment of party identifications.

A systematic disappointment from the established political parties, founded in anger, might, as well, be the base for the shaping of an anti-establishment political identification. The rise of simultaneously negative partisanships toward the mainstream parties does not necessarily lead to a party-system collapse. However, it can create an anti-establishment identification if it is not a mere rejection to the party system but it is sustained in self-perceptions associated with social stereotypes as regular party identifications. Anti-establishment political identifiers can also project their own social prototypes as any regular positive or negative partisanship.

It is important to differentiate between simple negative partisanship and an anti-establishment political identification (or "anti-establishment sentiments" or "anti-politician attitudes"). The latter is the addition of negative partisanships related to the established political parties. Actually, anti-establishment identifiers can be labeled as simple "independents," but they are detractors of the established political parties. For example, 61 percent of "independents" in the United States do not like either the Democratic or Republican parties (Klar & Krupnikov 2016). This distinction is not trivial because the literature has found different profiles among both groups. For example, while negative partisanship is positively correlated with electoral participation and forms of political participation, anti-establishment attitudes are associated with a decrease in turnout and an absence of partisanship (Caruana et al. 2015).

What are anti-establishment political identifiers made of? Rejection of established parties could create a political identity if it is defined in terms of belonging to a social group that opposes them. In this case, the crystallization of a political cleavage that divides society between those who feel represented by the political establishment and those who perceive themselves as excluded could allow the latter to create a personal connection that sustains over time. Actually, political cleavages involve the creation of political identities on each side of the divide (Ostiguy 2009). Accordingly, a populist dichotomist and Manichean view of society permits a polarization between two groups: An in-group of those perceived as belonging to the "honest people" as opposed to the out-group made up of the corrupted elite. This self-perception of the anti-establishment identifiers serves as a social prototype that presumably most resembles them. Populist sets of ideas are powerful "thin-ideological" glue for those identified with the systematic rejection of the political establishment. In this sense, we expect that anti-establishment identifiers also hold a populist worldview of society.

I distinguish between anti-political sentiments and an anti-establishment political identity. The former are psychological reactions during specific junctures while the latter is a mid-term political identification built on a social identity, regularly structured on populist appeals. When party-systems collapse, like in Peru in the early 1990s or Venezuela in the late 1990s, anti-political sentiments – expressed in voting preferences in favor of outsiders like Alberto Fujimori and Hugo Chávez, respectively – developed into anti-establishment identities that, in the long run, transformed into positive partisanships toward fujimorismo and chavismo. In other cases, like in contemporary Chile, anti-establishment political identities can endure without transforming into a positive identification.

"anti-dupolio" opposition to the two traditional coalitions has increased in the last decade without endorsing any political party.

Not all individuals develop a positive or negative political identification. Apartisans do not recognize themselves as part of any political group. They do not develop perceptions of belonging to in-group or sentiments of rejection to out-group. They are not organized around ideological tenets or are not attracted by populist appeals. Actually, I agree with theoretical expectations that consider that they are unable to position themselves in terms of the left-right continuum and that they reject populist appeals since the latter implies a form of politicization (Meléndez & Rovira 2019). They may share social attributes – especially belonging to specific cohorts – but, politically, they are disaffected. Apartisans are characterized mainly for their political indifference and for not having developed a sense of belonging to any political group. They do not reject the establishment; they are indifferent to it. Actually, by contrast, anti-establishment identifiers are highly politicized. By considering apartisans as a specific group of nonpositive partisans, I pretend to tackle a traditionally neglected aspect in the study of political linkages within elites and individuals: those who are not politically connected at all (Mair 2013).

In sum, my proposed conceptualization of apartisanship is more precise than previous efforts. It is not just a matter of political independence from the established parties (Dalton 2013). Although I agree with definitions of apartisans as those individuals who lack strong identification with in-group and, simultaneously, lack strong antipathies for out-group, I emphasize another two points. First, I differentiate apartisans from anti-establishment identifiers, which is a common confusion. As demonstrated previously, they represent two different profiles. Second, apartisanship is not a mere lack of positive or negative partisanship. It is also the lack of a politicized social stereotype. While (positive and negative) partisans and anti-establishment identifiers are based on social stereotypes, apartisans do not have a social reference group. Thus, they cannot position themselves as "independents" or opponents to the political establishment because they simply are not touched by politics. By treating apartisans as a discrete group, I propose to emphasize that politics has its own limits, and it is unable to reach all members of a community. Apartisans are politically orphans, and they are ok with this situation.

3.1 Measurement

An anti-establishment political identity is the addition of every negative partisanship related to the established political parties of a party system. Accordingly, this measurement should consider a previous step: Clarity about which political parties should be considered as part of the political establishment. In highly institutionalized party systems, this panorama is

Table 3 Measures of anti-establishment political identification and apartisanship in Latin America

Country and year	Anti-establishment ID	Apartisanship
Chile 2015	12.9	38.6
Brazil 2018	23.8	17.7
Honduras 2018	6.2	22.9
Argentina 2019	4.6	13.7

Source: UDP in Chile, Ipsos in Brazil, Borge & Asociados in Honduras, and Isonomía in Argentina.

evident. But when party systems are in flux – for example, when political parties lose electoral relevance frequently – it is very difficult to name the members of the party establishment. Due to this limitation, I conducted the proposed measurement of anti-establishment political identity for four of the studied cases: Chile 2015, Brazil 2018, Honduras 2018, and Argentina 2019 (Table 3). In the case of Chile 2015, I worked with the classification of two main traditional party coalitions: Nueva Mayoría (center-left) and Chile Vamos (center-right), based on previous works (Meléndez & Rovira 2019). These two coalitions have alternated in power since the return to democracy in 1990 and have settled a "duopolio." In the case of Brazil 2018, three political parties have dominated the electoral scene in recent decades: PT, PSDB, and MDB. This party hegemony in the Executive and Legislative has been characterized as "coalitional presidentialism." In the case of Honduras 2018, I considered the two members of the traditional bipartidism – Partido Liberal and Partido Nacional – as well as a new third force, LIBRE, a successful split from Partido Liberal. Finally, in the case of Argentina 2019, I included the study of the two main camps of "La Grieta" (the Crack): the peronista camp (including kirchnerismo)[14] and the PRO. In all four cases, anti-establishment party identifiers are those who hold simultaneously the negative partisanships of the respective established parties.[15]

According to the conceptualization of apartisanship, I consider this a residual category: all those individuals who lack any positive or negative partisanship. Based on the proposed operationalization, they might have

---

[14] Peronismo and kirchnerismo are two positive partisanships that intersect each other. For overlapping positive identities in the case of Argentina, see Cyr & Meléndez 2021.

[15] It is only possible to measure anti-establishment political identification in those party systems with established political parties. This has not been the case of Peru and Colombia, with very fluid party systems. In the case of Mexico, unfortunately, the measurement did not include the case of PRD, a traditional left-wing party. Without this case, it is not possible to have an adequate measurement of anti-establishment identity.

electoral preferences for candidates of party A for a public position X and for candidates of party B for public position Y, but they do not behave as loyal followers of party A or as constant detractors of party B. Therefore, I consider apartisans to be not only those individuals with no electoral preferences at all (e.g. individuals who answered "Don't Know" to the questions of the multi-item measurement) but also those with no coherent record of party sympathies or party antipathies. My proposed measurement is different from others that do not capture the absence of any type of partisanship. For example, Dalton's conceptualization of "apartisans" refers to "independents ... cynical about both (American) political parties" (Dalton 2013, p. 2), which actually resembles my suggested measurement of anti-establishment political identification. The measurement of partisanship used in this work goes in line with Samuels and Zucco's "nonpartisans:" those who lack strong antipathies for out-group and who lack strong identification with in-group (Samuels & Zucco 2018).

3.2 Anti-establishment Identifiers and Apartisans in Chile, Brazil, Honduras, and Argentina

Contemporary Chile, Brazil, Honduras, and Argentina are ideal settings to apply the proposed post-partisan typology and especially to show the differences between anti-establishment identifiers and apartisans. First, in the first three cases, their respective party systems have been associated with processes of PSI with relatively falling levels of volatility. The Chilean party system has been defined as a highly institutionalized one (Mainwaring et al. 2018) despite the unrootedness of most of its parties (Altman & Luna 2011). The Brazilian party system has been described as in the process of partial institutionalization (Mainwaring et al. 2018); however, it has advanced from an inchoate party system to an "uneven institutionalization." The Honduran party system has been characterized as a successful case of transformation from a traditional two-party system to a multiparty system with clearly defined and socially rooted parties (Romero 2019). Although the Argentinian party system has been deinstitutionalized (Gervasoni 2018), in the last few years, a dynamic of political polarization has made visible two distinct political camps (kirchnerismo and anti-kirchnerismo), and some authors have referred to bi-coalitionalism (Mauro 2018; Cruz 2019). These two political forces clearly represent the dominant players in the Argentinian political game, that is, the political establishment.

A clear and publicly recognizable party establishment is convenient for the measurement of party identifications and anti-establishment identification.

Acute electoral volatility in Latin America hinders the institutionalization of a party establishment. Only in countries that, despite volatility, can raise a notorious political establishment is it feasible to measure individuals who reject it. While it is very complicated to detect a clear political establishment in Peru or in Ecuador, since parties that control the political arena change from one election to the other; political establishments in Chile, Brazil, Honduras (and lately Argentina) have maintained control of the public agenda and electoral politics, despite party fragmentation and the emergence of new parties. Due to these considerations, it is reasonable to measure anti-establishment identification where there are clear establishments (like Chile, Brazil, and Honduras) and/ or where party competition is dominated and monopolized by recognizable partisan coalitions (like in contemporary Argentina).

At the same time, despite relative stability of party establishments in Chile and Brazil, they have experienced extreme pressure and stress lately. In the case of Chile, researchers have noticed signs of precariousness in the traditional "duopolio" (Luna 2017). However, a recent and surprising wave of social protests has cast more doubts about the representativeness of the Chilean party establishment. No political party – not even the newest left-wing coalition Frente Amplio – has capitalized the protests that demanded a new constitution. In Chile, the political establishment is clearly under pressure and there are no signs of recovery, while at the same time the rise of anti-establishment sentiments is evident. In the case of Brazil, the election of Jair Bolsonaro, who portrayed himself as an outsider, put an end to the electoral domination of PT during the previous four electoral cycles and interrupted the dynamics of the coalitional presidentialism controlled by PT. Although political scandals like the Lava Jato case involved parties from the whole ideological spectrum, public opinion reaction was focused on progressive PT. Accordingly, Bolsonaro's conservative right-wing anti-establishment discourse, mixed with strong positions on social issues (immigration, abortion, affirmative actions, among others) and pro-military issues (i.e. defense of the military dictatorship's heritage), was supported by 46 percent in the first round of the presidential election and by a 55 percent in the ballotage. Bolsonaro took advantage of anti-petismo as well as of a cultural backslash against progressive issues and social policies (Rennó 2020). Although the rise of his Social Liberal Party formed a new coalition with PSDB and MDB as minor partners, creating a new dominant alliance, there are signals that anti-petismo has evolved into a more generalized anti-partisan sentiment (Fuks et al. 2021).

In other cases, despite signs of deinstitutionalization or volatility, political parties control the political competition, and negative partisanships are channeled by the same political parties of the system. In these cases, the emergence of anti-establishment political identities composed by simultaneous rejection of the main political parties is marginal. In contexts where political parties are perceived as very distinctive from each other and not as part of the same shady deal, negative partisanships do not intersect in greater proportions. These are the cases of Honduras and Argentina, for example. In the case of Honduras, the unconstitutional re-election of Juan Orlando Hernández (Partido Nacional) in 2017 has represented a setback for the democratic regime. Social protests emerged through the movement of "anti-JOH" (referring to the president's name initials) but were channeled by the opposition parties, especially by LIBRE. In the case of Argentina, the space for an autonomous anti-establishment political identity has kept marginal, at least until 2019 elections, because polarization between kirchnerismo and anti-kirchnerismo is the building block of political identities. Argentinians interested in politics tend to take a political side on this profound confrontation.

Measurements of party identification, anti-establishment identification, and apartisanships were applied previously to the wave of social protests in Chile (in June 2015) and to the emergence of Bolsonaro in the electoral campaign in Brazil (in February 2018). Timing was appropriate in both countries. In the case of anti-establishment identification, we can measure it before its politicization via social movements (in Chile) or via the emergence of an extremist populist candidate (in Brazil). Although the proportions of anti-establishment identifiers might have increased due to the events mentioned, the original surveys conducted captured the nature and main characteristics of the nucleus of anti-establishment identification. In the case of apartisanships, the survey measures apprehend the extension of political apathy under contexts of acute pressures over the political establishments. By analyzing the ideological and sociodemographic characteristics of anti-establishment identifiers and apartisans, it is possible to better understand pressures over the establishments or their collapses.

In the cases of Honduras and Argentina, the applications of the measurements were during the contexts of decisive national elections: in December 2017– January 2018 in Honduras, just after the General Elections held in November 2017; and in October 2019, a month before the first-round presidential elections in Argentina. Electoral timing might undercount individuals categorized as anti-establishment identifiers, since elections encourage them to think about their political preferences. However, the proposed multi-item measurement intends to capture consistent party loyalties rather than mere voting preferences. Therefore, it reduces the impact of electoral contexts on partisan classifications. Moreover, anti-establishment sentiments and apathy have not vanished under electoral contexts. In the next sub-sections, I explore specific contextual factors associated with the shaping of anti-establishment identifiers and with the differentiation from apartisans in each of the four cases studied.

Table 4 First-round presidential elections results (1989–2017)

	1989	1993	1999	2005	2009	2013	2017
Concertación/ Nueva Mayoría	55.17	57.98	47.95	45.96	29.6	46.7	22.70
Alianza/Chile Vamos	29.40	24.41	47.51	25.41	44.06	25.03	36.64
				23.23			

Source: SERVEL.

3.2.1 Chile

After the return to democracy, two political coalitions have shared political power in Chile. Presidential candidates from the left-wing coalition (Concertación/Nueva Mayoría) have won five of the seven elections since 1989 (the first four consecutively, from 1989 to 2005), and the right-wing coalition (Alianza/Chile Vamos) have won the remaining two, both in ballotage and both with the same candidate, Sebastián Piñera. Although third-party forces turned out to be electorally competitive in some electoral episodes (Frente Amplio in the 2017 election obtained 20.27 percent, and Mayoría por Chile in 2009 obtained 20.14 percent), these two alliances have been the two most voted forces since the return to democracy until 2017 elections. (Table 4).

During this period, political competition between these two coalitions has been framed in ideological terms. However, over time there has been programmatic convergence. While progressive governments have adopted market-oriented policies inherited from the authoritarian regime with relative minor changes (Heneus 2005), the right-wing parties have adapted its programmatic discourse toward the necessity of market regulation, the expansion of the welfare state (Rovira 2019). Established political parties moderated themselves and started being perceived as indistinctiveness by the population (Bargsted & Somma 2016). This programmatic convergence and moderation were partly responsible for creating a dealignment process (Bargsted & Somma 2016) triggered by the parties' apparent brand dilution (Lupu 2015b). Chileans started a process of a gradual abandonment of political parties and a steady decline of partisanship (Bargsted & Maldonado 2018). But this dealignment process might have created a specific political identification based on the rejection of the establishment (Meléndez & Rovira 2019). For many Chileans, both coalitions responded to the same agenda. Relatively high levels of inequality and business interests linked to both coalitions have been perceived negatively by Chileans. For some authors, the perception of the entire establishment as business-oriented and as a perpetuator of inequality is a relevant reason linked to the increasing rejection of the establishment (e.g. Luna 2017). With no political alternatives and with a limited political supply, Chileans have not embraced massive membership of emerging political parties (e.g. Frente Amplio), but instead grew a group of anti-establishment identifiers, highly politicized but opposed to the moderate and convergent coalitions.

3.2.2 Brazil

Since 1945, Brazilian presidents have been required to build broad political coalitions in order to govern (except for the dictatorship period). Its multiparty political system has been categorized as one of the most fragmented globally (Mainwaring 1999). Its open-list proportional representation system encourages supporting candidates based on personalistic appeals rather than in-party linkages. As a result, the incumbent party has not held more than 25 percent of legislative seats (Pereira et al. 2008). Executive–legislative relations have developed amid the necessity of bargaining that implies going beyond ideological overlaps (Ames 1995).

From 1994 to 2014, Brazil's multiparty system has been dominated by PSDB and PT. The PT accessed the Executive in two consecutive periods (1994–1998, 1998–2002), and the PSDB in the remaining intervals (2002–2006, 2006–2010, 2010–2014, 2014–2018). The recurrence of these two parties as the most voted contributed to the institutionalization of the party system. Coalitional presidentialism (Presidencialismo de Coalizão) practiced in recent decades also included the participation of Partido do Movimento Democrático Brasileiro (PMDB), a pivot party that has been indispensable for every governmental coalition. Despite its importance, PMDB has not accessed federal power via elections. Its political cadres have historically played a relevant role forging agreements and benefiting from the perils of coalitional presidentialism (Table 5).

This coalitional presidentialism, however, has developed a negative dimension in order to survive. The steady increase of political fragmentation in Legislative branches (from seven relevant political parties in 1998 to thirteen in 2017 in the House of Representatives, and from four relevant political parties in 1998 to eight in 2017 in Senate) has directly affected the formation of coalitions. The necessity of expanding the number of associates led to increased

Table 5 First-round presidential elections results (1994–2014, Brazil)

	1994	1998	2002	2006	2010	2014
PT	27.0	31.7	46.44	48.61	46.91	41.59
PSDB	54.3	53.1	23.19	41.64	32.61	33.55

Source: Tribunal Superior Eleitoral.

clientelism and corrupted practices to build broad political agreements (Abranches 2018). The recent judicialization of Brazilian politics is the result of exposing malpractice for the first time to public scrutiny (Dallagnol 2017).

In recent years, coalitional presidentialism entered into a new phase characterized by the expansion of corrupt practices involving the active participation of public and private companies. First, public scandals (*Mensalão*) exposed illegal side payments to legislators as a mechanism of coalition management under permissive conditions (Pereira et al. 2008). Second, recent police investigations (*Operação Lava Jato*) of white-collar corruption (involving high-ranking officials) found a sophisticated system of bribes ("propinas") paid by businessmen in order to get public contracts. Thus, the coalitional presidentialism turned into a cooptational presidentialism. (Carazza 2018).

These political scandals involved the whole political establishment, across different ideological origins, and impacted citizens' confidence. Actually, party identification has recently dropped to low levels and there is evidence of citizen disaffection from political parties (Pavao 2015). Moreover, social protests led to increased nonpartisanship and weakening of support toward PT (Winters & Weitz-Shapiro 2014). The specialized literature has mainly focused on the decline of partisanship and the emergence of negative partisanship (Samuels & Zucco 2018). However, the slow collapse of the establishment may have nurtured an anti-establishment political identification, a systematic opposition to the practitioners of traditional coalitional presidentialism (Fuks et al. 2021).

3.2.3 Honduras

From the 1910s until the 2013 elections, Honduras has been characterized as a two-party system (e.g. Taylor-Robinson 2009). The Honduran Liberal Party and the Honduran National Party have dominated the political scene and have survived democratic interruptions and dictatorships (Morris 1984). Between the 1980 democratic transition and 2009 elections, they peacefully alternated in the presidency and built one of the most institutionalized party systems in Latin America (Romero 2019). The interaction of electoral and party institutions perpetuated caudillo politics within a democratic regime (Taylor 1996). Similarly to the other cases of two-party systems (e.g. Venezuela before Chávez) or two party coalitions (e.g. Chile after Pinochet), the two main political organizations ended up converging ideologically (Ajenjo Fresno 2007), and both parties represented the economic elite's conservative interests (Arancibia Córdova 1991). This regular alternation in office allowed the nurturing of partisan identifications, especially via clientelistic strategies (Taylor 2006).

Then-Liberal Manuel Zelaya's swing to the left after the 2009 elections altered the traditional partisan equilibrium. This shift to the left alienated the political and economic establishment that ended up overthrowing him from office (Meza 2015). Despite the reaction of the bipartisan establishment to repair the political equilibrium (Gonzáles-Ocantos et al. 2015), a third force emerged in the Honduran political scene. Since 2013, Honduras transitioned from a bipartisanship toward a three-party system due to the emergence of LIBRE, a left-wing split from the Liberals directed by Manuel Zelaya (Otero-Felipe 2013). Despite the fact that he has been disqualified from running for presidential office again, LIBRE has become the second force in Hondura's politics, displacing Liberals, and ended up winning the 2021 presidential elections (Table 6).

Honduras's party system successfully evolved from a bipartisanship to a multiparty system with notorious ideological differences among their members. Recent studies have shown clear programmatic differences between Partido Nacional (right-wing), Partido Liberal (center-right), and LIBRE (left-wing) (IUDPAS 2020). However, the coup *d'etat* against Manuel Zelaya in 2010, the constitutional interpretation that allowed José Orlando Hernández running for presidential re-election in 2017, and the accusations of fraud during those elections have created systematic repulsion of the political establishment. The decrease of electoral participation, the loss of credibility on elections as legitimate and impartial mechanism for appointing public officials, and the increasing certainty among citizens that electoral fraud had been committed in recent elections have contributed to the crisis of the establishment (Romero 2019). LIBRE has attempted to capitalize these anti-political sentiments, and, based on that, create its own positive party identification, which is higher (13.7 percent) than the partisanship of the original Liberal Party (9.7 percent). The successful emergence of a third political force might have contributed to the reduction of anti-establishment political identification.

3.2.4 Argentina

After the return to democracy in 1983, Argentinian politics was dominated by a bipartidism (McGuire 1995). From then onto the 1995 elections, Partido Justicialista (PJ) and Unión Cívica Radical (UCR) concentrated a majority of votes in both the Presidential elections and the Legislative elections. However, while PJ maintained important levels of support, UCR weakened progressively (Torre 2003). The political establishment formed by these two parties did not survive the end of the 1990s. Political instability and social unrest affected the party system's stability. It turned into a declining party system, with simultaneous processes of party fragmentation, denationalization of the party system, factionalization, and

Table 6 First-round presidential elections results (1981–2017, Honduras)

Party	1981	1985	1989	1993	1997	2001	2005	2009	2013	2017	2021
Partido Liberal	51.0	51.0	44.3	53.0	52.7	44.3	49.9	38.1	20.3	14.7	9.8
Partido Nacional	45.5	45.5	52.0	43.0	42.7	52.2	46.2	56.6	36.9	42.9	35.9
LIBRE									28.8	41.4	50.6

Source: CEDOH.

Table 7 Percentages of valid votes for Partido Justicialista and UCR (1983–1995)

Elections	1983	1985	1987	1989	1991	1993	1995
Presidential	91.9			79.7			67.0
Legislative	85.9	77.8	78.7	73.0	69.3	68.9	64.8

Source: Torre 2003

Table 8 First-round presidential elections results (2015–2019, Argentina)

Political party	2015	2019
Frente para la Victoria/Frente de Todos	37.1	48.2
Cambiemos/Juntos por el Cambio	34.2	40.3

Source: Cámara Nacional Electoral.

personalization within political parties and fluidity (Gervasoni 2018). The party system did not collapse completely presumably due to the resilience of peronism, which was able to forge societal links with traditional union organizations and urban informal sectors (Table 7) (Levitsky 2003).

Although it is a complex and volatile party system, it would be inaccurate to identify a political establishment in the voting dynamics of the last two Argentinian elections. The elections introduced a new version of the traditional peronism/anti-peronism divide (Nállim 2014), based on two political camps: kirchenismo and anti-kirchnerismo. Kirchnerismo is the left-wing faction that has dominated the peronism since Nestor Kirchner became president (2003) and its social support is grounded on the vindication of low-income citizens and anti-military sensibilities (Grimson 2019). PRO, on the other hand, emerged as a political project promoted by business sectors and the middle classes opposed to kirchnerismo (Vommaro 2017) and is in the process of forging its own partisanship (Baker & Dorr 2019). The division and polarization between these political forces is commonly known as "La Grieta," and it is assumed that most Argentinians identify as followers of one of these two political sides. The proposed measurement of anti-political establishment will allow us to know the proportions of individuals who do not belong to any of these camps because they reject both sides (anti-establishment) or because they are completely indifferent to them (apartisans; Table 8).

3.3 Data

I obtained the measurements of anti-establishment identifiers based on simultaneous negative partisanships related to the mainstream political parties in each country. Apartisans, on the other hand, are those individuals who do not belong to any of the positive or negative partisanship sets. Accordingly, in Chile in 2015, anti-establishment identifiers are those individuals who hold a negative partisanship toward Nueva Mayoría and a negative partisanship toward Alianza, and they correspond to 12.9 percent of the interviewed sample. Apartisans added up to 38.6 percent (Figure 8). In Brazil 2018, anti-establishment identifiers (anti-E area in Figure 9) are defined as the result of those individuals who simultaneously reject PT, PSDB, and MDB, which was 23.8 percent of the sample. Apartisans, all those individuals excluded from positive or negative partisanships, correspond to 17.7 percent (Figure 9). In the case of Honduras 2018, anti-establishment political identification corresponds to those who hold negative partisanships toward the Partido Nacional, Partido Liberal, and LIBRE, which totaled 6.2 percent of the sample (anti-E area in Figure 13). Surveyed individuals that do not hold any positive or negative partisanship reached 22.9 percent of the sample (Figure 13). Finally, the case of Argentina is special because anti-establishment identification is the result of the sum of three negative partisanships: anti-kirchnerismo, anti-peronism, and anti-PRO. However, anti-peronismo is a subset of anti-kircherismo, in the same line as kirchnerismo is a subset of peronism. Based on this intersection, anti-establishment identifiers are 4.6 percent of the sample (anti-E area in Figure 14), and apartisans are 13.7 percent.

Are anti-establishment identifiers substantially different from apartisans? It is a common mistake to confuse individuals who reject the establishment with those who have no political interest at all. The fact that they lack any positive partisanship does not mean that all of them are apathetic. In fact, anti-establishment identifiers are highly politicized since they are defined by their simultaneous rejection of the established parties, while apartisans are definitively far from politics. They do not connect positively or negatively with any political organization. In order to explore to what extent anti-establishment identifiers and apartisans are two different profiles, I explore two possible ideological articulations that might explain their respective cohesiveness: A traditional left-right programmatic preferences, and a "thin-ideology" composed by populist appeals. Logistical models considering every positive, negative, anti-establishment, and apartisan political identifications have been conducted for the four countries studied (Annex 1). I considered ideological self-positioning (in the conventional 1–10 scale) as a proxy for ideology and

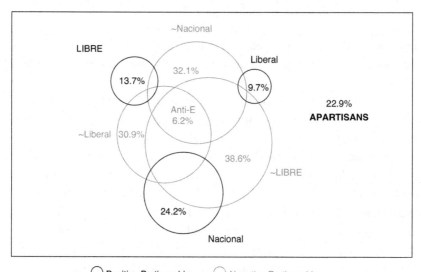

Figure 13 Different types of partisanship and their relative size in Honduras 2018

Source: B&A 2018

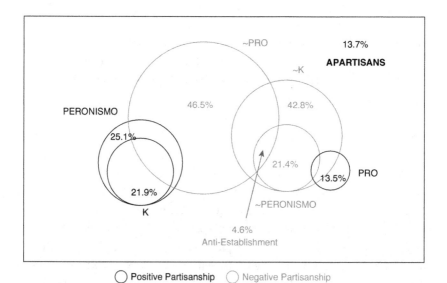

Figure 14 Different types of partisanship and their relative size in Argentina 2019

Source: Isonomía 2019

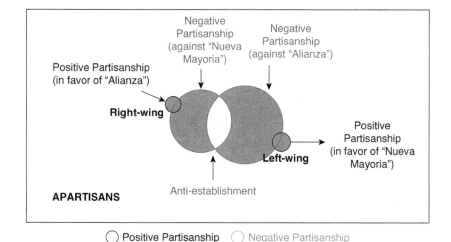

Figure 15 Ideological self-placement as predictor for political identifications in Chile 2015

a populist index for measuring populist appeals. Statistically significant results are shown in the following figures.[16]

In the case of Chile, as anticipated in Meléndez and Rovira (2019), anti-establishment identifiers and apartisans cannot be explained by conventional programmatic preferences. Ideological self-positioning efficiently explains positive and negative partisanships related to the traditional coalitions (Alianza and Nueva Mayoría) (gray intense areas in Figure 15) but not simultaneous negative partisanships and not the absence of positive or negative party ID (blank areas in Figure 15). However, populist appeals serve as ideological glue for negative partisans and anti-establishment identifiers (darker gray areas in Figure 16). These groups rank higher in the populist appeals scale. Therefore, it follows that, among apartisans, populist appeals are negatively associated. Apartisans are so politically disaffected that they reject any kind of politicization, including populism (lighter gray areas in Figure 16).

In the case of Brazil, I find a similar picture, with certain nuances. Ideological self-positioning efficiently explains every positive and negative partisanship.

---

[16] Sets are colored according to the following pattern. If, after conducting the respective logistic model, a political identity is statistically explained by ideological self-positioning, the corresponding set is painted in green (99 percent of confidence interval corresponds to intense green; 95 percent or 90 percent of confidence interval corresponds to light green). If a political identity is statistically and positively explained by the populist appeals index, the corresponding set is painted in yellow (99 percent of confidence interval corresponds to dark yellow; 95 percent or 90 percent of confidence interval corresponds to light yellow). And, if a political identity is statistically and negatively explained by the populist appeals index, the corresponding set is painted in blue.

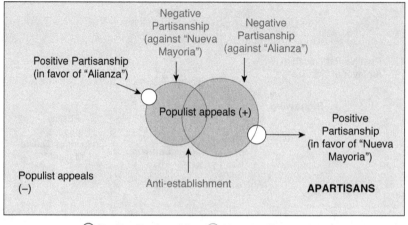

Figure 16 Populist appeals as predictor for political identifications in Chile 2015

As expected, PT partisans are left-wing hardcore followers, and PSDB's and MDB's followers are classified as right-wingers (although the relationship is statistically significant at 90 percent of confidence interval in the case of MBD's positive partisans). Negative partisanships are predicted in the expected ideological leanings (intense gray areas in Figure 17). A move to the right in the ideological scale increases the propensity of categorizing as an anti-petista, while a shift to the left in the same scale increases the propensity of qualifying as an anti-PSDB and as an anti-MDB. According to the logistical models performed, anti-establishment identifiers are explained by ideological self-positioning (intense gray areas anti-E in Figure 17). A move to the right in the ideological scale increases the propensity of being an anti-establishment identifier at a 95 percent confidence interval. Ideological tenets, though, do not help to explain apartisanship (blank area in Figure 17).

Populist appeals help explain petistas, every negative partisanship, anti-establishment identifiers, and apartisans. An increase in the index of populist appeals is positively associated with being a petista. Populist appeals, though, are not associated with other positive partisanships. Like in the case of Chile, an increase in the populist index increases the propensity of been anti-petista (although relationship is significant at 90 percent of confidence interval) (light gray area in Figure 18), been anti-PSDB, and been anti-MDB (statistically significant at 95 percent) (dark gray areas in Figure 18). As expected, anti-establishment identifiers are explained by their attraction to a populist worldview (anti-E area in Figure 18). Apartisans, on the other hand, are also explained by populist appeals, but on the opposite side of the spectrum. Brazilian

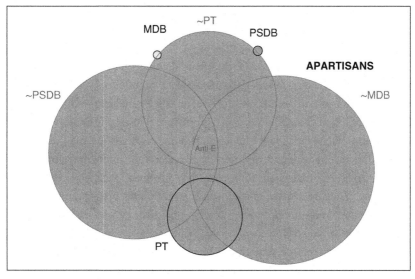

Figure 17 Ideological self-placement as predictor for political identifications in
Brazil 2018

Source: Ipsos 2018

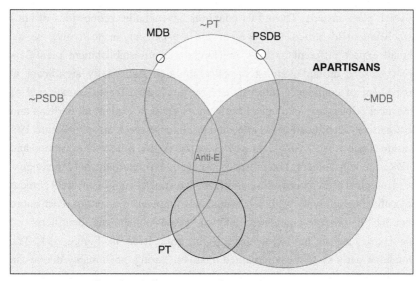

Figure 18 Populist appeals as predictor for political identifications in Brazil
2018

Source: Ipsos 2018

apartisans tend to reject any form of politicization, including populism (medium gray area in Figure 18). An increase in the populist index decreases the propensity to be categorized as apartisans.

In Chile and Brazil, anti-establishment identifiers are coalesced around populist appeals. They might have ideological preferences (Brazilian anti-identifiers are right-wingers), but they share this Manichean view of society based on their repulsion of the party establishment. By the time the surveys were conducted, anti-establishment identifiers had not endorsed any political party, but they were connected to politics by a concurrent animadversion to the partisan offer. Apartisans in both countries, however, lack any ideological positioning. They do not recognize themselves as having programmatic preferences, but they certainly are adversarial to populism. While populism might result attractive to the followers of certain political parties (e.g. PT in Brazil) or to negative identifiers (e.g. anti-Nueva Mayoría in Chile, anti-PSDB in Brazil), it definitively is rejected by apartisans. Chilean and Brazilian apartisans are averse to the Manichean political worldview that populism brings to the fore.

Chilean and Brazilian party systems have been in flux and the proportions of individuals in each of these two countries that are classified as anti-establishment identifiers are relatively high, especially in comparison to party systems like in Honduras and Argentina where political parties still capture positive partisanships. Those two countries have smaller proportions of anti-establishment identifiers (6.2 percent and 4.6 percent, respectively), so we should expect different profiles. In Honduras, anti-establishment identifiers are coalesced around populist appeals (although statistically significant at 90 percent of confidence interval) and by ideological tenets (same level of statistical relevance). Ideological preferences serve to explain all partisan and post-partisan identifications as expected (all intense green areas in Figure 19): Partido Nacionalista's followers are right-wingers, and followers of Liberal and LIBRE are left-wingers. Their respective negative counterparts hold the opposite ideological preferences (all relations are statistically significant at 99 percent of confidence interval). Although statistical significance does not reach more than the 90 percent confidence interval, anti-establishment identifiers and apartisans tend to be left-wingers (light gray areas in Figure 19). The Honduran party system has remained relatively strong, presumably due to the validity of ideological preferences to coalesce positive partisans, negative partisans, those who reject the establishment, and even those disaffected from politics (Figure 19).

While ideological tenets work as cohesive articulations among identifiers, populist appeals play a secondary role. Nacionalista followers are also explained by their rejection of populist appeals (medium gray area in Figure 20), while

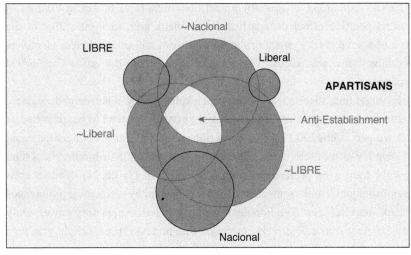

Figure 19 Ideological self-placement as predictor for political identifications in Honduras 2018

Source: B&A 2018

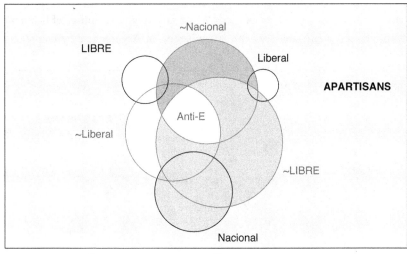

Figure 20 Populist appeals as predictor for political identification in Honduras 2018

Source: B&A 2018

Nacionalista's negative identifiers are characterized by their endorsement of populism (dark gray area in Figure 20). Negative LIBRE identifiers tend to reject populist appeals (medium gray area in Figure 20). The populist index has null effect on explaining anti-establishment identifiers (anti-E area in Figure 20) and its positive effect on apartisanships (blank area in Figure 20). In the case of a solid party system, differences between anti-establishment identifiers and apartisans are minor. They might even share the same ideological preferences.

In Argentina, ideological preferences explain every positive and negative partisanship. As expected, peronistas and kirchneristas tend to be classified as left-wingers, while PRO's followers as right-wingers. Anti-PRO identifiers tend to have left-wing preferences while anti-peronistas and anti-kirchneristas tend to hold right-wing preferences (dark gray areas in Figure 21). Neither anti-establishment identifiers nor apartisans are explained by ideological preferences (blank areas in Figure 21). Populist appeals have less explanatory power: Only anti-kirchnerismo is positively correlated with populist appeals (light gray area in Figure 22). Similarly, neither anti-establishment identifiers nor apartisans are coalesced by their support or rejection of a populist worldview. Where party systems are strong and have created programmatic links to society, populist appeals have less relevance. Consequently, anti-establishment identifiers and apartisans – those groups of individuals characterized by their rejection or apathy to a party system – tend first to be marginal groups and second to share similar ideological properties. While in Honduras anti-establishment identifiers and apartisans are both left-wingers, in Argentina they cannot be

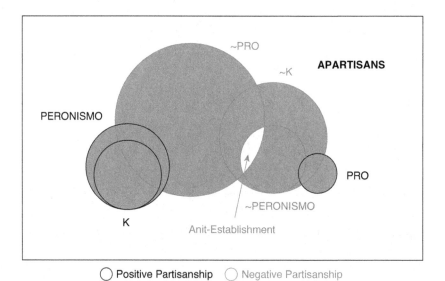

○ Positive Partisanship   ○ Negative Partisanship

Figure 21 Ideological self-placement as predictor for political identifications in Argentina 2019

Source: Isonomía 2014

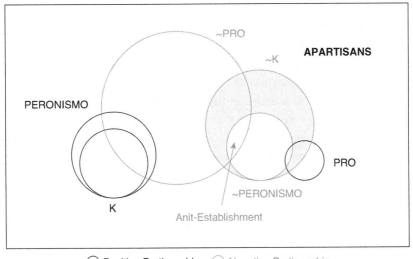

Figure 22 Populist appeals as predictor for political identifications in Argentina 2019

Source: Isonomía 2019

explained by ideological preferences and populist appeals only articulate Honduran apartisans.

After the application of the categorization of anti-establishment identifiers and apartisans in two types of party systems (institutionalized but socially uprooted party systems like Chile and Brazil, and deinstitutionalized but socially rooted party systems like Honduras and Argentina), we have demonstrated its usefulness to better understand rejection and apathy to the party establishment. In the former type, increasing disconnection between parties and society has alienated significant proportions of individuals. A group of them remain politicized but with a permanent aversion to the party establishment (anti-establishment identifiers); while another group remains apathetic with a structural indifference (apartisans). Anti-establishment identifiers, under these circumstances, have not coalesced around ideological tenants but have around populist appeals, independently of whether this populist worldview of society connects (Bolsonaro in Brazil) or not (Chile) with political leaders. Apartisans, on the other hand, reject any type of politicization, including ideological considerations and populist narratives. While anti-establishment identifiers share a populist "thin ideology" that works as a social identity that structures their anti-establishment sentiments as a permanent identification, apartisans reject populist appeals and completely lack any political identification.

Where political parties still connect with society – especially based on traditional programmatic linkages as the literature considers (Mainwaring & Scully 1995) – anti-establishment identifiers and apartisans are marginal groups. With the predominance of ideological connections, populist appeals lose explanatory power, and work as a complementary layer, especially to articulate negative partisanships (like anti-Partido Nacional in Honduras, and anti-kircherismo in Argentina). Overall, however, anti-establishment identifiers and apartisans are secondary players in political arenas dominated by partisan politics. In these cases, anti-establishment identifiers tend to lack any social identity that may structure them. In Honduras and Argentina, anti-establishment identifiers are not explained by populist appeals; and ideological considerations only connect with the Hondura's establishment defectors. Apartisans do not follow a pattern in these systems. In Honduras are explained by ideological considerations and populist appeals, but in Argentina they are not coalesced by ideology or populism. In any case, where positive partisanships are (still) solid, anti-establishment political identification and apartisanships are marginal for explaining party–citizens connections (Table 9).

Ideological appeals contribute to the social rootedness of the political parties. In socially uprooted party systems, anti-establishment identifiers tend to be disconnected not only from political parties but also from pro-grammatic linkages. Under these circumstances, populist appeals work as a cohesive articulator among those who hold an anti-establishment political identity. While apartisans also lack ideological connections, they tend to reject any form of politicization, even populism. Anti-establishment identifiers could be the raw material that indicate the likely emergence of populist leaders, like the case of Bolsonaro in Brazil, while apartisans might remain politically disaffected. In socially rooted party systems, anti-establishment identifiers and apartisans are marginal or less deleterious to the PSI. But when positive partisanship is in decline, anti-establishment political identity and apartisanship are more salient, and their effects on the prospects of the party system are harmful. Animosity and indifference,. respectively, erode the legitimacy of any party system.

4 Implications of Post-Partisan Political Identities

Post-partisan identities do not represent a recent phenomenon. The literature has traced the existence of negative partisanships and apartisanship since the origins of the conceptualization of positive partisanship. However, post-partisan

Table 9 Ideology and populism as articulators of anti-establishment political identity and apartisanship in Chile, Brazil, Honduras, and Argentina

| Party system | Country | Anti-establishment identifiers | | Apartisans | |
		Ideology	Populism	Ideology	Populism
Institutionalized but socially uprooted	Chile	No	Yes (Positive)	No	Yes (Negative)
	Brazil	No	Yes (Positive)	No	Yes (Negative)
Deinstitutionalized but socially rooted	Honduras	Yes	No	Yes	Yes (Positive)
	Argentina	No	No	No	No

identities have acquired unprecedented magnitudes in recent decades, especially in Latin America. In more than thirty years of experiencing democracy, Latin America has developed some forms of partisanship (Lupu 2015a), an identification that could be positive or negative, as well as anti-establishment identification. Focusing on positive partisanship produces a partial understanding of how individuals are attached to political parties. Therefore, we need to turn our attention to those individuals who are not positively linked toward political parties.

By focusing on post-partisan identities, we can better grasp a political phenomenon like party-building, partisan polarization, and PSI, which have traditionally assumed individuals dichotomously in terms of their partisanships (holding a positive partisanship or not). Unfortunately, we lack adequate data to test the presumably causal relationships between the different types of partisanship (and apartisanship) and the previously mentioned variables. However, based on the empirical data at the individual level regarding partisan and nonpartisan identifications and based on secondary sources, it is possible to notice some implications of nonpositive partisanships on party-building, different schemes of polarization based on different types of partisanships, and the consequences of post-partisanships on PSI. This section is devoted to questioning some assumptions of the party politics literature and to show the usefulness of the perspective of post-partisan political identities to shed light on the changes in the functioning of political parties in Latin America.

4.1 Party-Building

(Positive) partisanships have decayed in several Latin American countries because of the weakening of traditional political parties. Once strong and socially legitimate political parties have become marginal within their party systems, and new political parties have emerged with high expectations. Between 1978 and 2005, 307 new parties were formed in Latin America but only 11 have been successful in securing at least 10 percent of the vote in five or more consecutive national legislative elections and surviving after their founding leader's disappearance (Levitsky et al. 2016). A few have been able to employ their political resources to nurture their own and respective (positive) partisanship. Without a solid party identification, it is very difficult to build a political party.

Party-building is the process by which new political parties take root in society (Levitsky et al. 2016). In theory, the leaders of new political parties should craft their respective partisanship while they are constructing the emerging political organization. Crafting partisanship is part of the tasks of party-building. However, partisanship formation – as a galvanized set of sentiments and ideas – is not necessarily a top-down process, a translation from the elites to their followers. In fact, in the case of new organizations, we have seen in Latin America that nascent partisanships, positive or negative, pre-dated the efforts of party-building. Authoritarian successor parties have built their organizations based not only on organizational inheritance but also on previous political identities that represent nostalgia for past dictatorships (e.g. pinochetismo in Unión Demócrata Independiente (UDI) in Chile) or for former insurgency groups (e.g. Frente Sandinista de Liberación Nacional (FSLN) in Nicaragua). Political identities that precede the formation of political parties might be positive as well as negative, and, as we have explained, each of these partisanships can be autonomous from each other and, therefore, can contribute to party-building of new organizations independently. For example, what type of ideational resource might have been at the base of Partido por la Democracia (PPD) in Chile if not anti-pinochetismo? Is it possible to explain the creation of PRO in Argentina independently of anti-peronismo?

I propose to include the role of positive and negative partisanships in the discussion about party-building. Partisanships, in general, should be understood as political resources strategic to constructing new political parties. Partisanship, as a social identity, is a container of programmatic and ideological preferences, as well as a vehicle of sentiments and memories shared by the followers of the respective political party. For example, Levitsky and collaborators have considered that past violent conflicts play a role in successful party-building because sharing a conflictive past is a key element for building a political community (Levitsky et al. 2016). Extraordinary conflicts do not only produce party differentiation essential for brand development (Lupu 2015a) but especially foster partisan attachments. Militants and active members of political parties – holders of a common partisanship – share in the meaning of traumatic political experiences, conveyed through memories and emotions that adopt an in-group identification. According to Rosenblatt, party vibrancy is explained, among other factors, by this type of symbolic resources shared by party members that glue party organizations together (Rosenblatt 2018).

Intense political conflicts – such as civil wars, insurgencies, or dictatorships – divide society into two or more groups. These divisions can evolve into positive and negative partisanships. When explaining successful cases of party-building in Latin America, most cases originated in the representation of one of the sides of the division. Successful parties have turned this traumatic experience into raw material for crafting positive and negative party identifications. For example, in Chile, UDI and Renovación Nacional (RN) as authoritarian successor parties were confronted with pro-democratic parties (like PPD). On the one hand, UDI and RN have developed their own positive partisanships based on the representation of the heritage of Pinochet's dictatorship, but at the same time have included a negative partisanship related to anti-communism. Political parties aligned in the Chilean leftist coalition, like PPD, have developed their own positive partisanship based on the values of the democratic transition and at the same time based on anti-pinochetismo. Political conflicts can shape positive and negative partisanships that are valid resources for successful party-building, or for the survival and revival of parties after electoral collapse (Cyr 2017). But what happens when political conflicts divide societies into opposing camps that do not advance into institutionalized party organizations? Is every negative partisanship, produced by political conflicts, a political resource efficient for party-building?

In successful cases of party-building (and party survival), partisan elites cultivate complementary positive and negative partisanships. For example, the rise of PT in the 1980s in Brazil is explained by the forging of a partisan identity that positively connects worker unions and popular social movements with the emerging party organization, as well as a rejection of the military dictatorship's bureaucratic authoritarianism and its legacy. However, a negative partisanship by itself, not complemented by a corresponding positive partisanship, is very unlikely to evolve as a valid political resource for complete party-building. For example, intense opposition to authoritarian regimes in Venezuela and Peru has divided these societies into two camps (chavismo and anti-chavismo, and fujimorismo and anti-fujimorismo, respectively). While positive identification toward chavismo and fujimorismo can be considered as raw materials for strengthening political parties – even in hostile grounds for party-building like Peru – only ephemeral political parties have emerged from the corresponding anti-camps, dominated by negative partisanships.

On the one hand, chavismo and fujimorismo evolved from simple sympathies toward their respective historical leaders (Hugo Chávez and Alberto Fujimori) onto nascent partisanships, before helping to organize Partido Socialista Unido de Venezuela (PSUV) and Fuerza Popular, respectively. Both parties are considered as successful cases (although incomplete) of party-building (Levitsky et al. 2016). On the other hand, their corresponding negative partisanships – anti-chavismo and anti-fujimorismo – have been mobilized, on the streets and in the ballot box. In Venezuela, Primero Justicia, one of the main anti-chavista parties, has not been able to consolidate despite the prominence of its leader Henrique Capriles (presidential candidate in 2012 and 2013) and ended up divided. In Peru, anti-fujimorismo has been so strong that it has impeded the electoral victory of Keiko Fujimori in the last three elections (2011, 2016, and 2021). However, political parties that emerged based on anti-fujimorista sentiments – such as PNP, and PPK – are marginal and have almost disappeared.

Negative partisanship can be crucial in contesting authoritarianisms and influencing electoral results, but by itself it is not a sufficient condition for building political parties.

Extraordinary political conflicts can aspire to become foundational moments. When you have party-system collapses, corruption scandals that involve mainstream parties, and constitutional change movements, these create the conditions for profound political divisions that separate society between the defenders of the questioned establishment and its challengers. Anti-establishment political identity emerges under those scenarios, as multiple negative partisanships toward traditional parties. As in the case of negative partisanships by itself, anti-establishment identification needs to be complemented with a positive one to evolve into a successful case of party-building. Peruvian anti-establishment identifiers converted into fujimoristas in the 1990s as well as Venezuelan anti-establishment identifiers turned into chavistas a decade later. Populist politicians can shape anti-establishment identities into nascent partisanships in favor of their movements. Current Brazilian anti-establishment identifiers could become followers of Bolsonaro, but Chilean anti-establishment identifiers may not develop into a positive partisanship, despite their growth, precisely due to the absence of a populist agent. Populist agency is crucial for converting anti-establishment identification into a positive one. When this happens, prospects for party-building increase.

Is it possible to build political parties from apartisanship? Party-building is not exclusively a matter of will. Political agency has its limitations, especially when structuring a political party from scratch. As the specialized literature has stated, party-building efforts are facilitated by the existence of previous political conflicts, a climate of polarization, as well as political infrastructure inherited from nonelectoral organizations or previous authoritarian regimes (Levitsky et al. 2016). Apartisans are precisely individuals who lack these characteristics: They tend not to take sides in relation to political conflicts, are not ideologically mobilized, and tend not to belong to civic society organizations. Therefore, they are very unlikely to develop (positive or negative) partisanship, or to endorse political parties. Political agents' efforts to build political parties are normally targeted at individuals interested in politics, who are prone to develop positive or negative partisanships; not to apartisans, who are very unlikely to participate in party-building projects.

Party-building theory has not paid enough attention to the role of partisanship in the structuring of a new organization. Classical theory has considered parties as a given, and, consequently, has considered partisanship as the outcome of a top-down process of indoctrination from elites' followers. However, when dealing with the formation of new political parties, it is worth questioning how partisanship is crafted. Under these circumstances, partisanship should be considered as a political resource usable for party-building. In some cases, it can even be considered as a preexisting element, preceding the organization of the political party. But is it possible for partisanship to exist before the party? Yes. First, in an incomplete version, as a nascent partisanship (not necessarily cohesive in programmatic terms) or as a political ID related to a noninstitutionalized political movement (like fujimorismo in Peru or chavismo in Venezuela). Second, as a negative partisanship. Negative partisanships can work as a cognitive shortcut to create a share identification before the developing of a positive party ID. For example, most of the Argentinians who contributed to the formation of PRO shared anti-peronista sentiments. Third, anti-establishment identifications can also work as raw materials for party-building, especially with populist organizations. In this sense, populist agency is needed to convert this simultaneous rejection toward the mainstream parties to the share identity of a new (populist) party like chavismo and fujimorismo. (Apartisanship has null effect for party-building). In conclusion, positive partisanship, and post-partisan identifications (like negative partisanship and anti-establishment ID) should be pondered as conditions that facilitate the building of new political parties, especially if we consider a bottom-up process.

4.2 Partisan Polarization

Political polarization has been conceived as a situation in which political parties and/or the electorate are deeply divided and engaged in confrontational competition (Sartori 2005). Conventionally, a party system is conceived as polarized when the ideological extremes are occupied by active political parties, considering the distance between them along the left-right spectrum. However, partisan polarization is not exclusively ideological. Party systems might be divided around other types of cleavages that also polarize societies, like the cleave dividing populism and anti-populism, an orthogonal axis in relation to the traditional ideological dimension (Pappas 2014; Zanotti 2019).

Partisan polarization, based on ideological or populist divisions, implies a partition rooted in clashing social identities and therefore, can serve to forge and/or strengthen partisanships (Carothers & O'Donohue 2019). To some degree, polarization can be useful to reinforce party brands (Lupu 2015b), and help define in-group/out-group societal memberships that structure partisanships. The peronism/anti-peronism divide in Argentina is an archetypical case of how identification with/against a political party goes hand in hand with the definition of social identities (Carothers & O'Donohue 2019) on each side of the separation. Being a peronista or an anti-peronista implies more than mere programmatic preferences for political parties representing these camps, but also, a sense of belonging to social groups differently arrayed within the hierarchies of Argentinian society (Ostiguy 2009).

However, the extremes of the partisan polarization might not necessarily be organized around positive partisanships (e.g. Democrats vs Republicans in the United States). Partisan polarization can be structured in conflicts between positive and negative partisanships (e.g. fujimorismo vs anti-fujimorismo in current Peru), between two negative partisanships (e.g. anti-Nueva Mayoría and anti-Chile Vamos in current Chile), and between positive mainstream partisanships and an anti-establishment partisanship (e.g. PT vs anti-establishment in Brazil, during the rise of Bolsonaro). This is not a minor detail, since the types of partisanships on the fringes are relevant for understanding how the political system processes polarization.

The literature on partisan polarization supposes a scheme of confrontation between two socially rooted positive partisanships (e.g. Abramowitz 2010). When positive partisanships are dominant, the respective negative partisanships are subsumed within them. For example, Partido Nacional and LIBRE have polarized Honduras' party system since the fall of Manuel Zelaya in 2009 (Otero-Felipe & Rodríguez-Zepeda 2016). The Nacionalista partisanship (right-wing and conservative) has monopolized the opposition toward Zelaya; while the emergence of LIBRE (a progressive and leftist spin-off the Liberal Party) has represented anti-nacionalismo after the decay of Partido Liberal, and animadversion against the Nacionalista President Juan Orlando Hernández (the anti-JOH movement) (Rodríguez & González 2020). Both positive partisanships have confronted each other in the 2013, 2017, and 2021 elections. Despite the traumatic transition from a centenary bipartisanship toward a more plural-party system, Honduras' party system has remained highly institutionalized (Romero 2019). Under these circumstances, polarization around positive partisanships has contributed to distinguishing party brands and establishing social roots linked to political parties, even in the case of a new political party like LIBRE. Chile, during the hegemony of bi-coalitional system (1989–2013), belongs to this typology as well.

In a different scheme, partisan polarization might divide society into two distant extremes, one represented by a positive partisanship and the other by a pure negative partisanship. The positive partisanship normally corresponds to an organized political structure while the confronted pole might be a negative partisanship not linked with a positive partisanship and temporarily expressed by electoral vehicles. When this happens, polarization does clarify voter choice but is not as useful for strengthening (positive) party brands as the literature has assumed (Lupu 2015b). Polarization does help citizens distinguish parties which, in theory, facilitates the formation of party attachments (Lupu 2015a). But this is not necessarily true when one of the poles lacks the political resources for crafting a positive partisanship. Polarization between peronismo and anti-peronismo in Argentina has contributed to the formation of a social identity in each camp that has facilitated the emergence of anti-peronista parties like PRO (Vommaro 2017). However, the effects of polarization in party branding are not sufficient to strengthen positive partisanship within the "anti"-camp. Peruvian and Venezuelan politics have been polarized lately between fujimorismo/anti-fujimorismo and chavismo/anti-chavismo (e.g. Corrales 2005; Meléndez 2019). While positive partisanships and successful (although yet incomplete) party-building have emerged from the "pro" camp (Fuerza Popular from fujimorismo and PSUV from Chavismo), only ephemeral political parties have emerged from the "anti" camp: PNP and PPK from anti-fujimorismo, and Primero Justicia from anti-Chavismo. When one of the poles involved is a pure negative partisanship, party polarization does not automatically make people more likely to be positive partisans. A polarized negative partisanship (confronted with a polarized positive partisanship) is difficult to represent because the mandate for the politicians positioned in the "anti" camp is to impede rivals from accessing power (anti-fujimorismo) or to demolish them (anti-chavismo). Once these objectives are accomplished, the incentives for party-building decrease. Thus, party polarization between a positive partisanship and a negative partisanship does not bring desirable outcomes for democratic politics.

Another possible pattern of polarization is between two negative partisanships independent of positive partisanships. In this case of negative partisan polarization, both extremes of the electorate are articulated by anti-movements and might endorse political parties, although only circumstantially. Polarized citizens are not devoted in their hearts and minds to the political parties positioned on the extremes; instead, they are viscerally polarized against their rival pole, but not necessarily feeling represented by a political organization positioned on their side. This kind of setting creates the illusion that political parties that benefit electorally from polarization have loyal followers. Therefore, the party system might look stable, but political parties are not socially rooted. Under these conditions, polarization has not served to promote party brands or forge positive partisanships. Present-day Chile is a good example of this situation. Negative partisanship toward each of the traditional coalitions (Nueva Mayoría and Chile Vamos) has aligned voters in two camps. However, measures of partisanship in favor of these coalitions have consistently decreased to minimal levels. Chileans have voted for candidates from these two alliances since the return to democracy until the 2017 elections mainly due to the animosities toward what their rivals represented. In the last two general elections (2017 and 2021), new political organizations have emerged capitalizing negative partisanships: rightist Partido Republicano based on anti-Nueva Mayoría (or anti-comunismo) and leftist Frente Amplio, based on anti-Chile Vamos (or anti-pinochetismo). However, it is still too early to analyze the strength of their respective nascent partisanships.

Finally, another scheme considers polarization between a positive partisanship (especially related to mainstream parties) confronted with an anti-establishment identification. In this case, polarization divides the defenders of the status quo (structured in partisanships of traditional political parties) against their detractors (articulated around an anti-establishment ID). Based on the latter, a populist challenger might emerge, trying to capitalize on anti-establishment sentiments. This is the case of populist polarization structured on a populist/anti-populist cleavage (Zanotti 2019). The case of Brazil after the corruption scandals exemplifies how populist polarization against PT and traditional parties (PSDB, MDB) originated the electoral victory of Jair Bolsonaro.

By specifying the types of partisanships (and post-partisanships) involved in mass partisan polarization, we can advance on the discussion about the links between these concepts. Polarization reinforces partisanship (Lupu 2015b), positive and negative party identifications. This is not a minor precision, because polarization tends to have beneficial consequences (e.g. clarify voter choice, distinguishing party brands, strengthening party attachments) when two positive partisans antagonize each other. When polarization encompasses a negative partisanship in one or two of the poles, it intensifies the "anti" component, making it more difficult to nurture a positive partisanship among the negative partisans. In the cases that polarization encompasses an anti-establishment identification, it creates the conditions for populist enterprises.

4.3 Party-System Institutionalization

(Positive) partisanship, by itself, can work as a proxy of PSI at the individual level (Dalton & Weldon 2007). In the same vein, post-partisan identifications can help us to better understand un-institutionalized or low-institutionalized party systems. Negative partisanships might produce a relative stability at the party system level that is not explained exclusively by surviving positive partisanships. Individuals might still vote for established parties not because they support them, but because they express the "lesser of two evils." In addition, anti-establishment identities can allow us to understand the closeness to a party-system crisis – or even a party-system collapse – and the expansion of apartisanship can help us assume that not all individuals in a party system need to be positively or negatively connected to political parties. In order to explore these assumptions, it is pertinent to associate partisan and post-partisans identifications with the concept of PSI.

PSI is one of the most common concepts employed in order to understand the stability of the partisan establishment. It refers to the stable set of parties that interact regularly (Mainwaring et al. 2018). The first conceptualization of PSI considered four dimensions: party stability, party roots in society, party organization, and party legitimacy (Mainwaring & Scully 1995). Based on this definition, some empirical works found patterns that contradicted theoretical expectations, especially some stable party systems that had parties lacking in societal roots (Luna & Altman 2011; Zucco 2015). The reformulation of the definition moved away from conceptualizing party roots in society as an intrinsic dimension of PSI, and considered it, along with party organization and party legitimacy, as "building rocks" of PSI but not as part of the core concept. However, a question remained unanswered: why can patterns of electoral competition be stable even when parties do not have strong roots, organization, and legitimacy?

For some authors, parties' roots in society are an intrinsic aspect of PSI. According to Dalton and Weldon, partisanship is a valid measure of PSI from the standpoint of the public (Dalton & Weldon 2007). For others, strong connections between voters and parties generally underpin party stability (Seawright 2012; Lupu 2015a). However, these authors have referred to only one type of partisanship: positive party identification. Positive partisanship, however, is probably the best proxy for tackling party roots in society even though it is not the only type of partisanship that contributes to party system stability.

Mainwaring, Power, and Bizarro have made progress on identifying connections between voters and parties that are not captured by traditional measurements of partisanship in Brazil (Mainwaring et al. 2018). They tested whether voters have both latent sympathies and antipathies toward parties, and found that negative orientations toward political parties are an important predictor of voter choice (in combination with sympathies toward parties). By the inclusion of negative partisanship in the analysis of party stability we can move the needle forward on the understanding of apparent paradoxes of party stability without roots in society. It is not positive partisanship, which is contributing to stability; instead, it is their negative counterparts.

The analysis of the cases of Chile and Brazil precisely shows that these "stable but uprooted" party systems ground their stability on negative partisanships coalesced on ideological tenets. Anti-Nueva Mayoría and anti-Alianza in Chile, and anti-petismo, anti-PSDB, and anti-MDB represent solid ideological positions that guide individuals in shaping their political preferences accordingly. However, negative partisanships in these countries are also articulated by populist appeals. When simultaneous negative partisanships encourage an anti-establishment political identification based on a populist worldview of society, the strength of the disdain toward the establishment can lead to acute social unrest (like the 2019 social protests in Chile) or the emergence of a radical populist leader (Bolsonaro in Brazil). Both phenomena were unexpected if we consider the apparent partisan stability. In a context where there is no clear party establishment and political parties are in flux, like in Peru, negative partisanships cannot even help stabilize the party system. In extreme cases of party system deinstitutionalization, negative partisanships are predominant, but they lack ideological structures that make them endure over time.

In cases of (still) socially rooted political parties, party systems have reached certain levels of stability precisely due to the centrality of ideological connections linked to positive partisanships. That is the case in Honduras, despite the weakening of the traditional two-party system and in Argentina, amid party deinstitutionalization processes. In these arenas, most political parties have developed their respective positive partisanships based on programmatic positions, even though in some cases they may have also developed populist appeals (e.g. PT in Brazil). But ideological preference prevails. Negative partisanships do not intersect themselves in considerable proportions, so the magnitude of anti-establishment identification is not relevant. Moreover, anti-establishment identifiers are not even coalesced around populist appeals. Under these circumstances, anti-establishment political identification is not a hazard for party-system stability. When anti-establishment political identification is feeble, it does not endanger the social basis of PSI.

While anti-establishment identifiers jeopardize PSI, apartisans tend to be neutral. Not all citizens need to be connected to political parties. The fact that significant proportions of the populations are not shaped by any positive or negative partisanship does not threaten the legitimacy of the party system as anti-establishment identifiers do. Apartisans tend to lack ideological articulations and to repel any form of politicization, including populism. Political apathy does not lead automatically to massive protests or active rejection of the established political parties. Therefore, apartisans live in isolation from politics, and this apathy does not lead to relevant consequences to the stability of the party systems.

However, in the long run, negative partisanships, anti-establishment political identity, and apartisanship might be detrimental for democracy under specific circumstances. When negative partisanships are not subsumed by positive partisanships and remain autonomous, individuals do not get attached to political parties. Consequently, individuals' vote choice is not mainly due to their animosities toward rival parties. In this case, it is very difficult to build democratic representation for two main reasons. First, individuals do not necessarily endorse parties' programmatic platforms but instead seek parties that will distance themselves from their rivals. Second, individuals do not develop loyalties to the parties they vote for, and might end up abandoning them easily. Without programmatic representation and without partisan loyalties, negative partisanships do not contribute to forge accountability.

Anti-establishment identifiers are highly politicized but they do not endorse any political party. They might have developed ideological preferences but they also get attracted to populist appeals. Their rejection of the political establishment may evolve into a reaction against the democratic political regime or may develop into an illiberal understanding of democracy. Anti-establishment populist identifiers rarely endorse political parties with loyalty, so they tend to be extremely distrustful about politics. When they reject the establishment and mistrust political alternatives, they reject any alternative of representation. Their politicized participation might take violent repertoires or support radical candidates that might harm the prospects for democracy.

Apartisans are politically disaffected individuals who are indifferent to political parties. They tend not to communicate their programmatic preferences and social demands to the institutional channels, nor back political parties or rally against them. Democracy demands at least, a minimal level of citizen involvement in politics that apartisans lack. Settings in which negative partisans, anti-establishment identifiers, and apartisans represent significant shares of the population have serious difficulties (re)building democratic representation. They create a kind of vicious circle because these political identities' profiles are difficult to represent politically, and thus, they might remain outside of the partisans' channels. Democracies with negative identifiers, with anti-establishment identifiers, and with apartisans are very unlikely to satisfy citizen demands. Democracies need positive partisans to achieve their promises.

5 Concluding Remarks

There are alternative ways in which political parties connect to individuals. I have elaborated an extensive typology of political identities that goes beyond the regular categories based on positive partisanship and considers post-partisan identifications like negative partisanship, anti-establishment political identity, and apartisanship. This classification is based on the premise that positive partisanship is just one way – in decline in some countries, in flux in others – in which party attachments work at the individual level and that disdain toward parties can actually shapes negative partisanships. Moreover, the proposed typology also distinguishes those individuals who reject all established parties from those who lack any positive or negative partisanship. It captures the total aversion toward political parties (anti-establishment political identity) and distinguishes it from a more profound apathy (apartisanship). Based on a rigorous measurement conceived at the individual level, I have built this comprehensive classification of political identities. In contexts in which positive partisanships are in flux, this wide-raging typology is useful to understand what the specialized literature has diagnosed as scenarios of just "decay" or "absence" of (positive) partisanships.

The typology of political identifications that I have developed in this Element has the potential to explain fundamental topics in the study of partisan politics like party-building, partisan polarization, and PSI, among others. Although we lack the adequate empirical evidence to test relationships of causation between post-partisan identities and these variables, I employed findings from the cases studied to find some patterns as demonstrated in the previous section. Longitudinal evidence is needed to test if these findings will endure over time, although, theoretically, partisanships should be stable and long lasting. Data from Peru (2011–2021) provide confidence about it. Overall, the discipline can gain more precision in interpreting political processes by employing the perspective of partisan and post-partisan identifications. In the next lines, I propose how we can go further in that respective research agenda.

What can we say about the future of party attachments in Latin America? Based on the evidence presented, negative partisanship tends to have a reinforcing effect on positive partisanship. When both identifications complement each other, the prospects for social rootedness increase. For example, activists of political parties perform their partisanships (positive and negative) more vividly, not only by endorsing their candidates but also through energetic participation (Meléndez & Umpiérrez de Reguero 2021). Party vibrancy can be explained when party activists and party elites engender attachments to their followers nurturing both their positive partisanships in favor of their parties and negative partisanships against their historical rivals. We know that party vibrancy is nurtured by traumatic experiences (Rosenblatt 2018), and that party members and followers relive their disturbing experiences by keeping an intense repudiation of their adversaries. The prospects of vivid political parties, with links in society, depend on the development of negative partisanships coherent with their partisan subcultures.

Negative partisanship and anti-establishment identification can also become obstacles for the future of specific political parties. Several traditional political parties have accumulated rejections against them, solidified in long-lasting negative partisanships. Negative identifiers related to these parties have organized collectively against their rivals and have contributed to their demise. That is, for example, the case of anti-aprismo in Peru. When studying the resilience of traditional political parties, the literature has explained the survival and revival of old political parties based on the mobilization of political and ideational resources (Cyr 2017). However, traditional parties' resistance is not just a matter of internal factors, but also a result of pressures exerted from the environment. Negative partisanships (e.g. anti-aprismo in Peru) and anti-establishment identifications (e.g. anti-establishment against Acción Democrática and COPEI in Venezuela) have made the survival of the respective traditional parties very difficult, despite the parties' resources. Based on these records, we can hypothesize about parties' life expectancies.

Post-partisan identities (negative partisanship, anti-establishment identity, and apartisanship) are not normally considered when studying party systems at the individual level. When party systems are institutionalized, the literature conceives that most citizens are linked to political parties through a positive partisanship; when they are not, theories assume the dominance of apartisanship or anti-establishment identification (e.g. Dalton & Wattenberg 2002; Dalton 2013). The inclusion of negative partisanship in the picture, can shed light on the discussion of party system restructuring (Roberts 2015; Silva & Rossi 2018). Pure negative identifiers (those who lack any positive partisanship) represent those individuals excluded from representation, as the result of neoliberalism and truncated second reforms. Those negative identifiers do not endorse the mainstream political parties that defend the hegemonic economic model and might position themselves outside the dynamic of the party system or against it. However, in comparison to apartisanship, they are politicized and, consequently, demanding for their political incorporation. By investigating the programmatic preferences of negative identifiers and anti-establishment identifiers, we can have a better grasp about alternatives for social incorporation or reincorporation to the democratic representation. As discussed, a post-partisan perspective has a great potential for rethinking partisan politics in Latin America and other developing democracies.

Annex 1

Table A1 Ideological self-positioning and populist appeals as predictors for positive and negative identifications, anti-establishment identification, and apartisanship, based on logistic models, controlling by sociodemographics

Country and year	Identification	Percentage	Left	Right	Populism	Income	Age	Gender	Education	Zone
Argentina 2019	Peronismo	25.11	***			—			—	—
	Anti-peronismo	21.42		***		+++				
	Kirchnerismo	21.89	***			—			—	—
	Anti-kirchnerismo	42.8		***	+	+++	++			+++
	PRO	13.46		***		+++	+++			
	Anti-PRO	46.52	***			—				—
	Anti-Establishment	4.65					—			
	Apartisanship	13.71					—			
Brazil 2018	PT	19.83	***		+++	—				
	Anti-PT	43.79		***	+	+++		—		
	PSDB	2.96		***		—			++	++
	Anti-PSDB	56.88	***		+++	—		—		+++
	MDB	2.39		**	+++	—		—		
	Anti-MDB	61.87	***		+++					
	Anti-Establishment	23.80		***	+++					+++
	Apartisanship	17.70			—					

Table A1 (cont.)

Country and year	Identification	Percentage	Left	Right	Populism	Income	Age	Gender	Education	Zone
Chile 2015	NM	9.05	***				+++			+++
	Anti-NM	28.85		***	+++	+	+++	–		
	Chile Vamos	5.66		***			+++		+	+
	Anti-CHV	33.89	***		+++		+++			
	Anti-Establishment	12.90			+++					
	Apartisanship	38.60			—					
Colombia 2019	Uribismo	6.89		***	++		+		+++	
	Anti-uribismo	35.66	***		+++				+++	—
Honduras 2018	Nacional	24.18		***	—			++	–	+
	Anti-nacionalismo	32.1	***		+++		+++	—		++
	Liberal	9.74	***							
	Anti-liberalismo	30.9		***						+++
	LIBRE	13.71	***			++				
	Anti-LIBRE	38.59		***	—		+++	+		
	Anti-Establishment	6.21	*							
	Apartisanship	22.91	*		+					
Mexico 2018	PRI	8.61		***	++		+++	—		
	Anti-PRI	40.68	***		++	—	+++			
	PAN	8.55		**			+			
	Anti-PAN	31.16	**		+++		+++	—		
	MORENA	23.64						—		
	Anti-MORENA	18.59		**	—		++	++		

Group	Item	Value			
Mexico 2019	PRI	2.82	**		
	Anti-PRI	49.67			
	PAN	4.75	**		
	Anti-PAN	46.45			
	MORENA	24.31		+++	+++
	Anti-MORENA	7.3		—	—
Peru 2011	APRA	2.91	***		***
	Anti-APRA	56.51	***		
	Fujimorismo	10.05	**	+++	
	Anti-fujimorismo	39.55	***	+++	—
Peru 2016	APRA	4.92	*		
	Anti-APRA	54.19	*	+++	
	Fujimorismo	9.8			
	Anti-fujimorismo	34.9	***	+++	
Peru 2019	APRA	5.27	*		—
	Anti-APRA	66.51	**	+++	+++
	Fujimorismo	8.78	***	+++	—
	Anti-fujimorismo	60.69	**	+++	+++

Note: 1–10 Left–right self-positioning scale employed in all cases. Item nonresponse rates vary from 12 percent (Honduras 2018) to 34 percent (Chile 2015)

* statistically significant at 90 percent of confidence interval, **statistically significant at 95 percent of confidence interval, ***statistically significant at 99 percent of confidence interval

− negatively associated and statistically significant at 90 percent of confidence interval, —— negatively associated and statistically significant at 95 percent of confidence interval, ——— negatively associated and statistically significant at 99 percent of confidence interval

+ positively associated and statistically significant at 90 percent of confidence interval, ++ positively associated and statistically significant at 95 percent of confidence interval, +++ positively associated and statistically significant at 99 percent of confidence interval

References

Abedi, A. (2004). *Anti-Political Establishment Parties: A Comparative Analysis*. New York: Routledge.

Abramowitz, A. (2010). *The Disappearing Center: Engaged Citizens, Polarization and American Democracy*. New Haven, CT: Yale University Press.

Abramowitz, A. & Webster, S. (2018). Negative Partisanship: Why Americans Dislike Parties but Behave Like Rabid Partisans. *Advances in Political Psychology*. 39, 119–135.

Abranches, S. (2018). *Presidencialismo de coalizão: Raízes e evoluçao do modelo politico brasileiro*. São Paulo: Companhia Das Letras.

Ajenjo Fresno, N. (2007). Honduras: Un Nuevo gobierno liberal con la misma agenda política. *Revista de Ciencia Política*. 27, 165–181.

Ames, B. (1995). Electoral Rules, Constituency Pressures, and Pork Barrel: Bases of Voting in the Brazilian Congress. *The Journal of Politics*. 57 (2), 324–343.

Angell, A. (2007). The Durability of the Party System in Chile. In P. Webb & S. White, eds., *Party Politics in New Democracies*. Oxford: Oxford University Press, 275–304.

Arancibia Córdova, J. (1991). *Honduras: ¿Un Estado Nacional?* Tegucigalpa: Editorial Guaymuras.

Baker, A. & Dalton, D. (2019). Mass Partisanship in Three Latin American Democracies. In N. Lupu, V. Oliveros & L. Schimerini, eds., *Campaigns and Voters in Developing Democracies: Argentina in Comparative Perspective*. Ann Arbor, MI: University of Michigan Press, 89–113.

Baker, A., Sokhey, A., Ames, B. & Rennó, L. (2016). The Dynamics of Partisan Identification When Party Brands Change: The Case of the Workers Party in Brazil. *The Journal of Politics*. 78 (1), 197–213.

Baker, A., & Dorr, D. (2019). Mass Partisanship in Three. Campaigns and Voters in Developing Democracies: Argentina in Comparative Perspective, 89.

Bankert, A. (2021). Negative and Positive Partisanship in the 2016 US Presidential Elections. *Political Behavior*. 43(4), 1467–1485.

Bargsted, M. A. & Somma, N. M. (2016). Social Cleavages and Political Dealignment in Contemporary Chile, 1995–2009. *Party Politics*. 22 (1), 105–124.

Campbell, A., Converse, P., Miller, W. E. & Donald, E. (1960). *The American Voter*. New York: Wiley.

Bargsted, M. A., & Maldonado, L. (2018). Party identification in an encapsulated party system: The case of postauthoritarian Chile. Journal of Politics in Latin America, 10(1), 29–68.

Carazza, B. (2018). *Dinheiro, eleiçoes e poder: as engrenagens do sistema politico brasileiro*. São Paulo: Companhia das Letras.

Carothers, T. & O'Donohue, A., eds. (2019). *Democracies Divided: The Global Challenge of Political Polarization*. Washington, DC: Brookings Institution Press.

Carrión, J. (2006). The Fujimori Legacy: the rise of electoral authoritarianism in Peru. Penn State Press.

Caruana, N. J., McGregor, R. M. & Stephenson, L. (2015). The Power of the Dark Side: Negative Partisanship and Political Behaviour in Canada. *Canadian Journal of Political Science*. 48 (4), 771–789.

Castiglioni, R. & Rovira, C. (2017). Challenges to Political Representation in Contemporary Chile. *Journal of Politics in Latin America*. 8 (3), 3–24.

Centro de Estudios Públicos, CEP. *Estudio Nacional de Opinión Pública*. Number 84, December 2019

Contreras, G. & Navia, P. (2013). Diferencias generacionales en la participación electoral en Chile, 1988–2010. *Revista de Ciencia Política*. 33 (2), 419–441.

Converse, P., Miller, W., Rusk, J. & Wolfe, A. (1969). Continuity and Change in American Politics: Parties and Issues in the 1968 Election. *The American Political Science Review*. 63 (4), 1083–1105.

Corrales, J. (2005). In Search of a Theory of Polarization: Lessons from Venezuela, 1999–2005. *Revista Europea de Estudio Latinoamericanos y del Caribe*. 79, 105–118.

Cotler, J. & Grompone, R. (2000). *Fujimorismo: ascenso y caída de un regimen autoritario*. Lima: Instituto de Estudios Peruanos.

Cruz, F. (2019). *Socios pero no tanto: Partidos y coaliciones en la Argentina. 2003–2015*. Buenos Aires: Eudeba.

Cyr, J. (2017). *The Fates of Political Parties: Crisis, Continuity, and Change in Latin America*. Cambridge: Cambridge University Press.

Cyr, J. & Meléndez, C. (2016). Anti-Identities in Latin America: *Chavismo, Fujimorismo*, and *Uribismo* in Comparative Perspective. Paper presented at the 74th Annual Midwest Political Science Association Conference, Chicago, IL.

Cyr, J. & Meléndez, C. (2021). Overlapping Political Identities in Latin America: The Case of Kirchnerismo and Peronismo in Argentina. Mimeo.

Dallagnol, D. (2017). *A luta contra a corrupçao: A Lava Jato eo future de um pais marcado pela impunidade*. São Paulo: Sextante.

Dalton, R. (2013). *The Apartisan American: Dealignment and Changing Electoral Politics*. Thousand Oaks, CA: Sage.

Dalton, R. & Wattenberg, M. (2002). *Parties without Partisans: Political Change in Advanced Industrial Democracies*. Oxford: Oxford University Press.

Dalton, R. & Weldon, S. (2007). Partisanship and Party System Institutionalization. *Party Politics*. 13 (2), 179–196.

Fiorina, M. (1981). *Retrospective Voting in American National Elections*. New Haven, CT: Yale University Press.

Fuks, M., Ribeiro, E. & Borba, J. (2021). From Antipetismo to Generalized Antipartisanship: The Impact of Rejection of Political Parties on the 2018 Vote for Bolsonaro. *Brazilian Political Science Review*. 15 (1), e0005.

Gervasoni, C. (2018). Argentina's Declining Party System: Fragmentation, Denationalization, Factionalization, Personalization, and Increasing Fluidity. In S. Mainwaring, ed., *Party Systems in Latin America: Institutionalization, Decay, and Collapse*. Cambridge: Cambridge University Press, 134–156.

Gonzáles-Ocantos, E., Kiwiet de Jonge, C. & Nickerson, D. (2015). Legitimacy Buying: The Dynamics of Clientelism in the Face of Legitimacy Challenges. *Comparative Political Studies*. 48 (9), 1127–1158.

Green, D., Palmsquist, B. & Schickler, E. (2006). *Partisan Hearts and Minds: Political Parties and the Social Identities of Voters*. New Haven, CT: Yale University Press.

Greene, S. (2004). Social Identity Theory and Party Identification. *Social Science Quarterly*. 85 (1), 136–153.

Grimson, A. (2019). *¿Qué es el Peronismo? De Perón a los Kirchner, el movimiento que no deja de conmover la política Argentina*. Buenos Aires: Siglo XXI.

Grompone, R. & Degregori, C. (1990). *Elecciones 1990: demonios y redentores en el nuevo Perú, una tragedia en dos vueltas*. Lima: Instituto de Estudios Peruanos.

Haime, A., & Cantú, F. (2022). Negative Partisanship in Latin America. *Latin American Politics and Society*, 64(1), 72–92.

Hawkins, K. A., Riding, S., & Mudde, C. (2012). Measuring populist attitudes.

Hawkins, K. & Rovira, C. (2017). What the (Ideational) Study of Populism Can Teach Us, and What It Can't. *Swiss Political Science Review*. 23 (4), 526–542.

Heneus, C. (2005). Las coaliciones de partidos: ¿un uevo scenario para el sistema partidista chileno? *Política: Revista de Ciencia Política*. 45, 67–68.

Huddy, L. (2001). From Social to Political Identity: A Critical Examination of Social Identity Theory. *Political Psychology*. 22 (1), 127–156.

IUDPAS (Instituto Universitario en Democracia Paz y Seguridad). (2020). *Percepción Ciudadana sobre Inseguridad y Victimización en Honduras*. Tegucigalpa: Universidad Nacional Autónoma de Honduras.

Kitschelt, H., Hawkins, K., Luna, J. P., Rosas, G. & Zechmeister, E. (2010). *Latin American Party Systems*. Cambridge: Cambridge University Press.

Klar, S. & Krupnikov, Y. (2016). *Independent Politics: How American Disdain for Parties Leads to Political Inaction*. Cambridge: Cambridge University Press.

Levitsky, S. (2003). *Transforming Labor-Based Parties in Latin America: Argentine Peronism in Comparative Perspective*. Cambridge: Cambridge University Press.

Levitsky, S., Loxton, J., Van Dyck, B. & Domínguez, J. (2016). *Challenges of Party-Building in Latin America*. Cambridge: Cambridge University Press.

Levitsky, S. & Roberts, K., eds. (2011). *The Resurgence of the Latin American Left*. Baltimore, MD: Johns Hopkins University Press.

Luna, J. (2016). Delegative Democracy Revisited: Chile's Crisis of Representation. *Journal of Democracy*. 27 (3), 129–138.

Luna, J. (2017). *En Vez del Optimismo*. Santiago: Catalonia-CIPER.

Luna, J. & Altman, D. (2011). Uprooted but Stable: Chilean Parties and the Concept of Party System Institutionalization. *Latin American Politics and Society*. 53 (2), 1–28.

Lupu, N. (2015a). Partisanship in Latin America. In R. Carlin, M. Singer & E. Zechmeister, eds., *The Latin American Voter: Pursuing Representation and Accountability in Challenging Contexts*. Ann Arbor, MI: University of Michigan Press, 226–245.

Lupu, N. (2015b). Party Polarization and Mass Partisanship: A Comparative Perspective. *Political Behavior*. 37, 331–356.

Mainwaring, S. (1999). *Rethinking Party Systems in the Third Wave of Democratization: The Case of Brazil*. Stanford, CA: Stanford University Press.

Mainwaring, S., Bizzarro, F. & Petrova, A. (2018). Party System Institutionalization, Decay, and Collapse. In S. Mainwaring, ed., *Party Systems in Latin America: Institutionalization, Decay, and Collapse*. Cambridge: Cambridge University Press, 218–234.

Mainwaring, S. & Scully, T., eds. (1995). *Building Democratic Institutions: Party Systems in Latin America*. Stanford, CA: Stanford University Press.

Mair, P. (2013). *Ruling the Void: The Hollowing of Western Democracy*. London: Verso.

Manrique, N. (2009). *Usted fue Aprista: Bases para una historia crítica del Apra*. Lima: Pontificia Universidad Católica del Perú.

Mauro, S. (2018). Coalition Politics in Federalized Party System: The Case of Argentina. In A. Albala & J. M. Reniu, eds., *Coalition Politics and Federalism*. New York: Springer, 113–128.

McGuire, J. (1995). Political Parties and Democracy in Argentina. In S. Mainwaring & T. Scully, eds., *Building Democratic Institutions: Party Systems in Latin America*. Stanford, CA: Stanford University Press, 200–248.

Medeiros, M. & Noel, A. (2013). The Forgotten Side of Partisanship: Negative Party Identification in Four Anglo-American Democracies. *Comparative Political Studies*. 47 (7), 1022–1046.

Meléndez, C. (2019). *El Mal Menor: Vínculos Políticos en el Perú posterior al Colapso del Sistema de Partidos*. Lima: Instituto de Estudios Peruanos.

Meléndez, C. & Rovira, C. (2019). Political Identities: The Missing Link in the Study of Populism. *Party Politics*. 25 (4), 520–533.

Meléndez, C. & Rovira, C. (2021). Negative Partisanship Towards the Populist Radical Right and Democratic Resilience in Western Europe. *Democratization*. 28(5), 949–969

Meléndez, C. & Umpiérrez de Reguero, S. (2021). Party Members and Activists in Latin America. In H. E. Vanden and G. Prevost, eds., *Oxford Research Encyclopedia of Politics*. Oxford: Oxford University Press.

Meza, V. (2015). *Diario de la conflictividad en Honduras, 2009–2015: Del golpe de Estado a las marchas de las antorchas*. Tegucigalpa: CEDOH.

Morgan, J. (2011). *Bankrupt Representation and Party System Collapse*. University Park, PA: Penn State University Press.

Morgan, J. & Meléndez, C. (2016). Parties under Stress: Using a Linkage Decay Framework to Analyze the Chilean Party System. *Journal of Politics in Latin America*. 8 (3), 25–59.

Morris, J. (1984). *Honduras: Caudillo Politics and Military Rulers*. Boulder, CO: Westview Press.

Murakami, Y. (2007). *El Perú en la era del Chino: La política no institucionalizada y el pueblo en busca de un salvador*. Lima: Instituto de Estudios Peruanos.

Nállim, J. (2014). *Las raíces del antiperonismo: Orígenes históricos e ideológicos*. Buenos Aires: Capital Intelectual.

Ostiguy, P. (2009). The High and the Low in Politics: A Two-Dimensional Political Space for Comparative Analysis and Electoral Studies. *Kellogg Institute Working Paper*, No. 360.

Otero-Felipe, P. (2013). El sistema de partidos de Honduras tras la crisis política de 2009: ¿El fin del bipartidismo? *Colombia Internacional*. 79, 249–287.

Otero-Felipe, P. & Rodríguez-Zepeda, J. (2016). Honduras: Continuidad en la agenda de gobierno en un nuevo contexto partidista. *Revista de Ciencia Política*. 36 (1), 195–217.

Palacios-Valladares, I. & Ondetti, G. (2018). Student Protests and the Nueva Mayoría Reforms in Chile. *Bulletin of Latin American Research*. 38 (5), 638–653.

Pappas, T. (2014). *Populism and Crisis Politics in Greece*. London: Palgrave Macmillan.

Pavao, N. (2015). *The Failures of Electoral Accountability for Corruption: Brazil and Beyond*. PhD Dissertation, University of Notre Dame.

Pereira, C., Power, T. & Raile, E. (2008). Coalitional Presidentialism and Side Payments: Explaining the Mensalao Scandal in Brazil. *Occasional paper*, No. BSP-03.

Rennó, L. (2020). The Bolsonaro Voter: Issue Positions and Vote Choice in the 2018 Brazilian Presidential Elections. *Latin American Politics and Society*. 62 (4), 1–23.

Roberts, K. (2015). *Changing Course in Latin America: Party Systems in the Neoliberal Era*. Cambridge: Cambridge University Press.

Rodríguez, G. & González, L. (2020). Honduras 2019: persistente inestabilidad económica y social y debilidad institucional. *Revista de Ciencia Política*. 40 (2), 379–400.

Romero, S. (2019). Democracia bajo tensión, elecciones cuestionadas y quiebre del bipartidismo: Honduras (1980–2019). In J. Castellano & S. Romero, eds., *Encrucijadas de la Democracia en Honduras y América Central*. Tegucigalpa: IUDPAS, 205–250.

Rose, R. & Mishler, W. (1998). Negative and Positive Party Identification in Post-Communist Countries. *Electoral Studies*. 17 (2), 217–234.

Rosenblatt, F. (2018). *Party Vibrancy and Democracy in Latin America*. Oxford: Oxford University Press.

Rovira Kaltwasser, C. (2019). La (sobre) adaptación programática de la derecha chilena y la irrupción de la derecha populista radical. *Colombia Internacional*. (99), 29–61.

Ruhl, M. (2010). Honduras Unravels. *Journal of Democracy*. 21 (2), 93–107.

Samuels, D. & Zucco, C. (2014a). Crafting Mass Partisanship at the Grass Roots. *British Journal of Political Science*. 45 (4), 755–775.

Samuels, D. & Zucco, C. (2014b). Lulismo, Petismo, and the Future of Brazilian Politics. *Journal of Politics in Latin America*. 6 (3), 129–158.

Samuels, D. & Zucco, C. (2018). *Partisans, Antipartisans, and Nonpartisans: Voting Behavior in Brazil*. Cambridge: Cambridge University Press.

Sartori, G. (2005). *Parties and Party Systems: A Framework for Analysis*. Colchester: ECPR Press.

Schedler, A. (1996). Anti-Political Establishment Parties. *Party Politics*. 2 (3), 291–312.

Scully, T. (1992). *Rethinking the Center: Party Politics in Nineteenth and Twentieth Century Chile*. Stanford, CA: Stanford University Press.

Seawright, J. (2012). *Party-System Collapse: The Roots of Crisis en Peru and Venezuela*. Stanford, CA: Stanford University Press.

Segovia, C. (2009). ¿Crisis de la política en Chile? Percepciones y valoraciones sobre los partidos. In *La Sociedad de la Opinión: Reflexiones sobre encuestas y cambio politico en democracia*. Santiago: Ediciones Universidad Diego Portales, 197–224.

Silva, E. & Rossi, F. (2018). *Reshaping the Political Arena in Latin America: From Resisting Neoliberalism to the Second Incorporation*. Pittsburgh, PA: University of Pittsburgh Press.

Somma, N., Bargsted, M., Disi, R. & Medel, R. (2020). No Water in the Oasis: The Chilean Spring of 2019–2020. *Social Movement Studies*. 20(4), 495–502.

Tanaka, M. (1998). Los espejismos de la democracia: el colapso de un sistema de partidos en el Perú, 1980–1995, en perspectiva comparada. Lima.

Tanaka, M. (2005). *Democracia sin partidos: Perú 2000–2005*. Lima: Instituto de Estudios Peruanos.

Taylor, M. (1996). When Electoral and Party Institutions Interact to Produce Caudillo Politics: The Case of Honduras. *Electoral Studies*. 15 (3), 327–337.

Taylor, M. (2006). La política hondureña y las elecciones de 2005. *Revista de Ciencia Política*. 26 (1), 114–124.

Taylor-Robinson, M. (2009). Honduras: Una Mezcla de Cambio y Continuidad. *Revista de Ciencia Política*. 29 (2), 471–489.

Tironi, E. & Agüero, F. (1999). ¿Sobrevivirá el Nuevo Paisaje Político Chileno? *Estudios Públicos*. 74, 151–168.

Torcal, M. & Mainwaring, S. (2003). The Political Recrafting of Social Bases of Party Competition: Chile, 1973–95. *British Journal of Political Science*. 33 (1), 55–84.

Torcal, M. & Montero, J. R., eds. (2006). *Political Disaffection in Contemporary Democracies: Social Capital, Institutions, and Politics*. New York: Routledge.

Torre, J. C. (2003). Los huérfanos de la política de partidos. Sobre los alcances y la naturaleza de la crisis de representación partidaria. *Desarrollo Económico*. 42 (168), 647–665.

Valenzuela, S., Scully, T. & Somman, N. (2007). The Enduring Presence of Religion in Chilean Ideological Positionings and Voter Options. *Comparative Politics*. 40 (1), 1–20.

Vommaro, G. (2017). *La larga marcha de Cambiemos: La construcción silenciosa de un proyecto de poder*. Buenos Aires: Siglo XXI.

Weisberg, H. (1980). A Multidimensional Conceptualization of Party Identification. *Political Behavior.* 2, 33–60.

Winters, M. & Weitz-Shapiro, R. (2014). Partisan Protesters and Nonpartisan Protests in Brazil. *Journal of Politics in Latin America.* 6 (1), 137–150.

Zanotti, L. (2019). *Populist Polarization in Italian* Politics, *1994–2016: An Assessment from a Latin American Anaylitical Perspective.* PhD Dissertation, University of Leiden.

Zechmeister, E. & Corral, M. (2013). Individual and Contextual Constraints on Ideological Labels in Latin America. *Comparative Political Studies.* 46 (6), 675–701.

Zucco, C. (2015). Estabilidad Sin Raíces: La Institucionalización del Sistema de Partidos Brasileño. In M. Torcal, ed., *Sistemas de Partidos en América Latina: Causas y Consecuencias de su Equilibrio Iestable.* Buenos Aires: Siglo XXI, 78–107.

Acknowledgments

I would like to acknowledge the useful comments from Cristóbal Rovira Kaltwasser, Lisa Zanotti, Matías Bargsted, and two anonymous reviewers. I also want to thank Ariel Becerra for his statistical assistance and Lizette Crispín for editing the graphics. I acknowledge support from Agencia Nacional de Investigación y Desarrollo-Chile (SIA Project SA77210008 and FONDECYT Regular Project 1220193) and from the Centre for Social Conflict and Cohesion Studies (COES; CONICYT/FONDAP/151330009). Finally, this work was benefited from the Research Excellence Fellowship sponsored by Central European University CEU/HESP Visiting Fellowship.

Cambridge Elements ☰

Politics and Society in Latin America

Maria Victoria Murillo
Columbia University

Maria Victoria Murillo is Professor of Political Science and International Affairs at Columbia University. She is the author of Political Competition, Partisanship, and Policymaking in the Reform of Latin American Public Utilities (Cambridge, 2009). She is also editor of Carreras Magisteriales, Desempeño Educativo y Sindicatos de Maestros en América Latina (2003), and co-editor of Argentine Democracy: the Politics of Institutional Weakness (2005). She has published in edited volumes as well as in the American Journal of Political Science, World Politics, and Comparative Political Studies, among others.

Tulia G. Falleti
University of Pennsylvania

Tulia G. Falleti is the Class of 1965 Endowed Term Professor of Political Science, Director of the Latin American and Latino Studies Program, and Senior Fellow of the Leonard Davis Institute for Health Economics at the University of Pennsylvania. She received her BA in Sociology from the Universidad de Buenos Aires and her Ph.D. in Political Science from Northwestern University. Falleti is the author of Decentralization and Subnational Politics in Latin America (Cambridge University Press, 2010), which earned the Donna Lee Van Cott Award for best book on political institutions from the Latin American Studies Association, and with Santiago Cunial of Participation in Social Policy: Public Health in Comparative Perspective (Cambridge University Press, 2018). She is co-editor, with Orfeo Fioretos and Adam Sheingate, of The Oxford Handbook of Historical Institutionalism (Oxford University Press, 2016), among other edited books. Her articles on decentralization, federalism, authoritarianism, and qualitative methods have appeared in edited volumes and journals such as the American Political Science Review, Comparative Political Studies, Publius, Studies in Comparative International Development, and Qualitative Sociology, among others.

Juan Pablo Luna
The Pontifical Catholic University of Chile

Juan Pablo Luna is Professor of Political Science at The Pontifical Catholic University of Chile. He received his BA in Applied Social Sciences from the UCUDAL (Uruguay) and his PhD in Political Science from the University of North Carolina at Chapel Hill. He is the author of Segmented Representation. Political Party Strategies in Unequal Democracies (Oxford University Press, 2014), and has co-authored Latin American Party Systems (Cambridge University Press, 2010). In 2014, along with Cristobal Rovira, he co-edited The Resilience of the Latin American Right (Johns Hopkins University). His work on political representation, state capacity, and organized crime has appeared in the following journals: Comparative Political Studies, Revista de Ciencia Política, the Journal of Latin American Studies, Latin American Politics and Society, Studies in Comparative International Development, Política y Gobierno, Democratization, Perfiles Latinoamericanos, and the Journal of Democracy.

Andrew Schrank
Brown University

Andrew Schrank is the Olive C. Watson Professor of Sociology and International & Public Affairs at Brown University. His articles on business, labor, and the state in Latin America have appeared in the American Journal of Sociology, Comparative Politics, Comparative

Political Studies, Latin American Politics & Society, Social Forces, and World Development, among other journals, and his co-authored book, Root-Cause Regulation: Labor Inspection in Europe and the Americas, is forthcoming at Harvard University Press.

Advisory Board

Javier Auyero, *University of Texas at Austin*

Daniela Campello, *Fundação Getúlio Vargas*

Eduardo Dargent, *Universidad Catolica, Peru*

Alberto Diaz-Cayeros, *Stanford University*

Kathy Hoschtetler, *London School of Economics*

Evelyne Huber, *University of North Carolina, Chapel Hill*

Robert Kaufman, *Rutgers University*

Steven Levitsky, *Harvard University*

Antonio Lucero, *University of Washington, Seattle*

Juliana Martinez, *Universidad de Costa Rica*

Alfred P. Montero, *Carlton College*

Alison Post, *University of California, Berkeley*

Gabriel Vommaro, *Universidad Nacional de General Sarmiento*

Deborah Yashar, *Princeton University*

Gisela Zaremberg, *Flacso México*

Veronica Zubilaga, *Universidad Simon Bolivar*

About the Series

Latin American politics and society are at a crossroads, simultaneously confronting serious challenges and remarkable opportunities that are likely to be shaped by formal institutions and informal practices alike. The Elements series on Politics and Society in Latin America offers multidisciplinary and methodologically pluralist contributions on the most important topics and problems confronted by the region.

Cambridge Elements ≡

Politics and Society in Latin America

Elements in the Series

Printed in the United States
by Baker & Taylor Publisher Services